AN INVISIBLE WORLD:

Revealing the Mysterybehind the World of Jinn

ISBN: 1-4392-0384-9
ISBN-13: 9781439203842

Visit www.booksurge.com to order additional copies.

AN INVISIBLE WORLD

Table of Contents

An Invisible World

INTRODUCTION

The Unseen. What do we know about it? Thousands of books and hundreds of films have been produced depicting it. The sole undisputable fact about it is that the reality of this invisible world is shrouded in confusion and mistaken common notions. At the outset, it is not the aim to be presumptuous by stating that this work is presented in a manner and approach that is different. We will be embracing diverse aspects and issues closely connected with the unseen world, based on either religious or academic sources, or both.

This book is not based on fables or myths, nor is it a work of fiction or the product of an overactive imagination. It is, however, a genuine study looked at from various aspects and based on the writer's personal experience and analysis over a period of twenty years. Research and meticulous attention to detail have been preserved with the inclusion of beneficial sources of reference taken from the Qur'an, the Bible, and teachings embodied in other religions, even if only passing reference is made.

In addition to this, it is indeed the intention of this work to share the information contained herein with the small group of related pioneers in this field. This includes those who have the ability to communicate with the Jinn either directly or through a medium.

An unmistakable reaction was glaringly apparent during the time these observations were made. This was the grief and suffering, bordering on the unbearable, caused by the interference of these creatures of the unseen world in the lives of human beings.

It is not unheard of, although it has not become a commonplace practice, to have society in general brand those who involve themselves or dabble in this hidden world as uncivilized or backward. Nevertheless, it is understood that the right to label or hold to such a perception is the right of all. Whatever the case, each individual has the free will to believe in this mysterious world or not.

Some of the ideas put forward in this book may be strange or unfamiliar to the reader. This is probably due to the fact that they are rarely discussed in detail. They may also be considered by some as extremely sensitive and too controversial to be discussed openly.

The general understanding among people is that Jinn are creatures with which they are familiar. It should be added, however, that many assume them to be creatures such as ghosts, ghouls, vampires, and various other names and terms, depending on the terminology given by a particular language or culture. Whatever the case, the reality of the matter is that they originate from a single type of being.

Taken from the perspective of human history, it is very difficult to locate any complete any comprehensive reference that specifically examines the world of Jinn or supernatural beings.

An analogy of this could be made as to when a person wishes to give a detailed explanation regarding the horse. For those who are totally familiar with the world of the horse, it would be not too difficult a task to discuss them incorporating all relevant and correct facts.

On the other hand, those who are inexperienced and unfamiliar with even the smallest details of the equine world, as the experienced horse breeder is, would certainly find subjects such as the habits of a horse, what makes it agitated or happy, etc., and all such matters quite difficult to understand, let alone to discuss.

In short, this example demonstrates that the more we have a connection with the animal kingdom, the easier it will be to study, discuss and understand. Nevertheless, if we apply our example to the Jinn and the invisible world, there is, however, quite a difference.

Jinn are highly complex and mysterious creatures. In reality, whatever occurs in their world becomes extremely difficult to accept or believe if human logic or rational thinking is applied. Yet despite this, the phenomenon of their existence has manifested itself in almost all beliefs and creeds embraced by humanity.

With regard to the information that is known thus far, the world of the Jinn is not a territory that is easy to explore or venture into deeply, not even for one who aims to reveal the vast secrets of the unseen world.

It is on this basis it must be said that there is no person who can arrogantly claim that he knows the world of the Jinn intimately; no one at all, including the writer.

The writer has put his utmost effort, based on his knowledge and experience, into explaining the facts regarding their world with absolute clarity and from diverse aspects and points of view.

The writer states clearly that he himself is not a person who claims to understand this invisible world perfectly and reiterates that no human can declare such a statement. He commenced this research in 1980 due to several reasons.

Armed with very elementary knowledge of the Jinn's world, we may at least be familiar with something of their history, background, identity, types, characteristics, habits, and various other aspects of these beings created by Allah the Almighty, who come from a different dimension but share the same universe as us.

Taken from another important viewpoint, some understanding of the Jinn and their world may provide us with the necessary advice and direction that could, at some point, prove vital in our lives.

It should be stressed that certain detailed information presented in this book may be difficult for some individuals to accept. Although this may be the case, the information is totally genuine and based on facts.

A further analogy may be compared here regarding belief in Heaven and Hell. It would not be an exaggeration to state that most people on the face of the earth believe in their existence. Yet it is totally impossible to see either of these places with the naked eye. The same comparison may be applied to the Jinn. Indeed, their existence has been pre-ordained in the same manner.

Despite this, however, the ability to see and experience the Jinn and the unseen world has notable exceptions. There is a small group of human beings who have been given the capability to perceive them with the naked eye.

These include children (usually under the age of five), people suffering from mental problems, people who are unconscious, acute drug addicts experiencing hallucinations, the insane, and animals. In certain circumstances with Allah's permission, it is not improbable that the opportunity to experience the same could be known by anyone—even by the reader— unintended, unplanned and unexpectedly.

As an introduction to the topics studied in this book, proofs from religious sources will be included. These will serve to demonstrate the essential fact that the Unseen and religious guidance cannot be separated. Nowadays the existence of supernatural beings is difficult for some people to accept, as their existence cannot be scientifically proven. Nevertheless, religious guidance is the only way to learn about the unseen world. *Wallahu a'lam* (Allah knows best).

Allah has bestowed certain Jinn with powers and abilities that are not possessed by humans: among them are the powers to move very fast, fly, appear in different forms, and possess other abilities that are difficult for the human mind to understand. It is generally known from a story in the Qur'an that a type of Jinn called an *'Ifrit* made a promise to Prophet Sulaiman to bring him the throne of Balqis, the Queen of Saba' in Yemen, in the time it took him to get up from his seat. There was, however, a man among them who had knowledge of the revealed Book, who possessed power much greater than that of the 'Ifrit Jinn:

"An 'Ifrit of the Jinn said: 'I will bring it [the throne] to thee before thou rise from

thy council: indeed I have full strength for the purpose, and may be trusted.' Said one who had knowledge of the Book: 'I will bring it to thee before the twinkling of an eye.' Then when [Sulaiman] saw it placed before him, he said: 'This is by the grace of my Lord! To test me whether I am grateful or ungrateful! And if any is grateful, truly his gratitude is [a gain] for his own soul; but if any is ungrateful, truly my Lord is Free of all Needs, Supreme in Honor!'"
(Surah An-Naml: 39–40)

The Qur'an also describes the Jinn's speed and ability to fly when they desire to ascend to certain places in the heavens. They used to have the ability to steal a hearing of the secrets of heaven in order to know about matters that were going to happen in the future. After the Prophet Muhammad was appointed a Messenger, this opportunity was permanently closed to the Jinn and devils with evil intentions:

"'And we the Jinn pried into the secrets of heaven; but we found it filled with stern guards and flaming fires. We used, indeed, to sit there in hidden stations, to steal a

hearing, but any who listens now will find a flaming fire watching him in ambush.'"
(Surah Al-Jinn: 8–9)

In a similar light, there is a narration regarding Al-Harith Ad-Dimashqi, who rose in Syria during the governance of 'Abdul-Malik ibn Marwan, claiming to be a prophet. With the aid of Jinn and devils, he possessed the power to make his body impenetrable to weapons. Following his capture by the Muslims to be executed, an individual drew his spear and attempted to stab him, but was unable to do so, on account of his power. 'Abdul-Malik ibn Marwan said to the man who tried to execute Al-Harith, "This occurred because you did not mention the Name of Allah while you speared him." So the man speared him a second time, but mentioning Allah's Name first, and this time the false prophet was finished off.

The narration above clearly indicates that the power of impenetrability was evidently practiced during the bygone era of the Islamic governance. In addition to impenetrability, other kinds of supernatural knowledge and magic were practiced by this sorcerer who claimed to be a prophet. Therefore it would not be surprising if we should see certain extraordinary abilities by those practitioners of witchcraft who claim to be special individuals. Their aim is to influence others to become their followers.

Another narration describes how a sincere and obedient servant of Allah had the power to perform actions that went beyond the acceptance of rational human thought, due to his close relationship to Allah the Almighty.

It is narrated by Imam Baihaqi in *Shu'abul-Liman* that Abu Muslim, or 'Abdullah ibn Thaub, came to Medinah after the Prophet passed away and missed the honorable opportunity to meet with him. At this time, one of the Prophet's *Sahabah* (Companions), Abu Bakr As-Siddiq had been appointed the first Caliph of Islam to lead after the demise of the Prophet. 'Abdullah ibn Thaub lived until the time of Yazid ibn Mu'awiyyah.

Among the stories narrated about him, it was said that one day Aswad al-'Ansi Al-Kadh'dhab said to him, "Do you witness that I am a prophet of Allah?" 'Abdullah ibn Thaub replied, "I refuse to listen to you." He then said, "Do you witness that Muhammad is the Prophet of Allah?" He replied "Yes." Following this, Aswad commanded his followers to light a blazing fire and cast

'Abdullah into it. They came back to see what happened to him, only to find him still alive and performing prayer inside the fire, which had become cool. He was unharmed by the fire and bore no sign of burns. Not long after, 'Umar, who had heard of his arrival in Medinah, summoned 'Abdullah to sit with him and Abu Bakr. He said to him, "Praise be to Allah who saved your soul so that he could show me a servant of Allah from Muhammad's *Ummah* (nation) who was tortured in the same manner as Prophet Ibrahim."

In reality, these extracts from the Qur'an and Sunnah presented here leave the strong impression that the phenomena of the unseen can be better understood through sources of religious guidance.

In the same light, it may be said the unseen world is synonymous with the beliefs and creeds of humankind. Therefore, the significance of religion cannot be underestimated in the explanation and clarification of phenomena that are grossly restricted if we apply the understanding of human logic and rationale.

Before we delve even deeper into the mystery of the unseen world, let us first look into the meaning of the word "unseen." In

Arabic, the word *ghaib* means "the opposite of something that is seen."

From an etymological point of view, the Unseen are those matters that cannot be perceived by the five senses.

It is, however, clear to us that the unseen world is a world that can be felt and seen, and its existence may be experienced by the five senses. Belief in the unseen is one of the pillars of *Iman* (faith) that constitutes the essential primary characteristics which define the people of *Taqwa* (God-consciousness), as mentioned in Surah Al-Baqarah verse 3:

"Who believe in the unseen, are steadfast in prayer..."

The unseen world is a very broad issue that encompasses diverse aspects embracing human religious belief and faith. In essence, although humankind has never witnessed them with their own eyes, we adhere to belief in Allah, Angels, Heaven, Hell, the soul, *Barzakh* (the world of the dead prior to Judgment) and Jinn; all of which are unseen.

There are a considerable number of Muslims who possess confused beliefs regarding the unseen world, regarding it solely as issues connected with Jinn and devils. It is a common belief that if someone claims to have the ability to communicate with Jinn or devils, this means that they understand the unseen world fully. The reality, however, is that the knowledge possessed by humankind about the Unseen is extremely minimal.

Rasulullah, who was chosen by Allah Himself, did not possess the knowledge of nor could he experience the Unseen such as Heaven, Hell, the spirit, *Barzakh* and Jinn with the senses, except by Allah's permission as a *Mu'jizah* (prophetic miracle) during his mission of *da'wah* (to invite to Islam) in spreading goodness among humankind and bringing mercy to the worlds. An example of this is the events surrounding the times he received revelation, whether indirectly or directly. Other examples are the event of *Isra' and Mi'raj* (the Night Journey), or when he saw the Angel Jibril and received revelation from Allah the Almighty through Jibril. All of these special events came about with Allah's permission and will. Regarding this, Allah the Almighty decreed in Surah Al-A'raf, verse 188:

Say: "I have no power over any good or harm to myself except as Allah willeth. If I had knowledge of the Unseen, I should have multiplied all good, and no evil should have touched me: I am but a warner, and a bringer of glad tidings to those who have faith."

With regard to the creation of Heaven and earth, and the spirit of living beings, Allah states:

"I called them not to witness creation of the Heavens and the earth, not (even) their own creation."
(Al-Kahf: 51)

He, Most High, also states:

They ask thee concerning the spirit. Say: "The spirit is of the command of my Lord. Of knowledge it is only a little that is communicated to you (O men!)."
(Al-Isra': 85)

The extent to which people have the ability to see Jinn in their true form depends on the aid of the Jinn themselves. This may even reach the level of being able to penetrate deep into their world and witnessing things not normally seen with the naked eye.

In addition to this, there are others who possess the ability to see and communicate with Jinn, based on either a desire to form such a connection or due to certain powers that the individual has gained from the Jinn. In reality, this power is not genuine, but a form of trickery from the Jinn. It follows that the unseen world perceived by an individual is limited to boundaries defined by his respective Jinn. These boundaries are, in fact, far restricted compared to the actual reality of the Unseen.

It is known that there are persons who can see and communicate with Jinn, but not based on knowledge related to the Unseen. Their respective Jinn appear as a result of magic in the various forms of hideous creatures or even beautiful beings accompanied by halos or shining light. These apparitions are, in fact, a form of trickery used by devils against humankind. There are certain people who can see Jinn or communicate directly with them due to the aid of the Jinn themselves. There are even types of Jinn who abduct humans in order to transport them to their world.

In almost all situations, we find ample supporting evidence that indicates that the power and extraordinary ability possessed by an individual to see and communicate with supernatural things, in reality, cannot be affected without the assistance and support of Jinn and devils. It should be noted that they have the ability to see humankind, whereas in normal situations, humankind cannot see them.

In Surah Al-A'raf, Allah explains to us that Jinn can see humankind, but humankind cannot see Jinn:

"...for he (Satan) and his tribe see you from a position where ye cannot see them..."
(Al-A'raf: 27)

Shaikhul-Islam, Ibn Taymiyah, when asked about this verse, commented: "Whatever is contained in the Qur'an regarding Jinn being able to see humankind, whereas humankind cannot see Jinn, is an established truth that demonstrates that they see humankind from a certain position where humankind are unable to see them."

From one angle, his statement illustrated a situation that became a reality. During

Ibn Taymiyah's life, he was active in carrying out therapy for people afflicted by Jinn. He witnessed various experiences himself while applying treatment to patients disturbed by Jinn or devils.

If a person has the ability to see Jinn, there are two possible reasons. One, the individual is a pious person who is close to Allah the Almighty and is given the ability by Him. Or two, the individual has gained the ability due to the aid and trickery of the Jinn, whose true aim is to misguide humankind.

It is absolutely clear that the ability of this first category of individual has not been gained due to learning, knowledge being transferred, or an inheritance from another individual. This type of ability is not the kind that can be used for show, entertainment, or display to others.

The ability of the second category of individual, however, is something that is sought after, learned, and may be passed on to others. This knowledge is impossible to gain except through a bond, either in the form of companionship or a "master and slave" relationship, with the Jinn and devils. It is another manifestation of Jinn trickery that may occur at any time or place. In truth, the reality of the Unseen is only within Allah's knowledge. For this very reason, human understanding and knowledge in connection with the unseen world is, indeed, extremely minuscule.

It is imperative for Muslims to hold onto correct sources that explain issues and information related to the Unseen. These sources can only be the Qur'an and Sunnah of Allah's Prophet. With the exception of these two sources, all else is deviant teaching and astray from correct guidance.

Islam wholeheartedly rejects stories or news regarding the past or future, pertaining to which is hidden from human sight, related by practitioners of magic or soothsayers who claim to read the future. All of this is rejected as it constitutes baseless, vague, and inconceivable information brought by Jinn and devils through connections between them and these people. Jinn possess their bodies and then whisper suggestions to them, claiming these issues to be secrets of the unseen world. In fact, the whole scenario is a form of deceit and trickery designed to drag humankind down to the level of *shirk* (polytheism).

This situation has been described in a *Sahih* (authentic) Hadith related by Abu Hurairah. The Prophet said:

> "When Allah decrees the command in the Heavens, the Angels beat their wings in obedience to His decree. The (sound of the) decree is like sound of a chain (being dragged) across rocks. The noise is deafening (to the extent they fall into a swoon from fear). After the feeling of fear leaves them, they ask each other, 'What has been commanded by your Lord?' They reply, 'The word of Truth. And He is Most High, Most Great.' At that moment, those (devils) who steal a hearing (of revelation) listen.

> "When the one who steals a hearing listens to the word (decree), he passes it on to the one beneath him, who in turn passes it on, and so forth until it reaches the mouth of the sorcerer or soothsayer. At times, some of the Jinn and devils who steal a hearing are hit by shaft of fire before they can pass on the word (decree). At times, they are able to pass on the news before the shaft of fire hits them. Therefore, one word of truth heard in this manner is

mixed with a hundred lies by the sorcerer or soothsayer."

People who visit soothsayers or shamans believe in the predictions and advice given by them. Certainly a part of what they declare is true, on account of the knowledge they have gained of the Unseen from the Jinn and devils. Yet it is certain with the small amount of knowledge of the Unseen whispered to them by the devils and Jinn, they duly add to and fabricate hundreds of similar lies to these unsuspecting people.

Al-Bukhari and Muslim narrates from A'ishah, who said:

"I said, 'O Prophet of Allah, we see soothsayers normally predict things and then these things actually happen.'

"He replied, 'The word heard by the Jinn is indeed the truth, which he then whispers into the ear of his companion. He, in turn, adds to it 100 lies.'"

Allah states in the Qur'an:

"...but any that gains a hearing by stealth, is pursued by a fiery comet, bright (to see)."
(Al-Hijr: 18)

It is evident to us from this verse that among the Jinn scattered over the face of the earth is a group that attempt to steal information and news of the Heavens. Following this, the news obtained by those Jinn and devils becomes the source of information used by mediums, soothsayers, and astrologers, not excluding practitioners of magic, to predict events and happenings that will occur in the future.

Soothsayers, mediums, astrologers, sorcerers and shamans usually receive inspiration or guidance in the form of whispered suggestions from devils, either directly or through specific rites or rituals.

It is not unusual for them to accustom themselves to practicing strange or weird rituals. These include isolating themselves for certain periods of time in places such as graveyards, fasting for long periods of time, or sacrificing animals with the intention of feeding the supernatural being. These are just some brief examples of various rites or rituals they perform that go against human norms.

Allah declares in the Qur'an:

"He (alone) knows the Unseen, nor does He make anyone acquainted with His Secrets. Except a messenger whom He has chosen: and then He makes a band of watchers march before Him and behind Him."
(Al-Jinn: 26–27)

It is imperative that humankind, particularly the Muslim *Ummah* (nation), recognizes and always remembers that absolute knowledge pertaining to all matters of the Unseen is possessed by Allah the Almighty alone. Notwithstanding this, at certain times Allah the Almighty may wish to unveil a portion of unseen matters and permit them to be seen by His chosen servants such as Prophets, Messengers or *Auliya'* (Muslim Saints). These special visions are bestowed to enable them to carry out the responsibility of spreading the message of Islam throughout the earth.

Satan has been the enemy of humankind since the beginning of time and will be an enemy forever. In effect, the devils and Jinn who follow Iblis (Satan) will not cease to assail humankind with various types of ruses, trickery and evil—from all directions and angles. This will continue until humankind is exhausted and finally surrenders to the forces of evil.

Humankind has continually been reminded to be on its guard in this world. Life is brief and full of risks. We are exposed all the time to the path of deviation, as a result of the deceit and evil preyed upon us by the minions of Iblis, the Jinn and devils.

"O ye people! Eat of what is on earth, lawful and good, and do not follow the footsteps of Satan, for he is to you an avowed enemy."
(Al-Baqarah: 168)

In short, the doors to evil and the risk of falling into the realm of misguidance are very great. Jinn and devils will endeavor unceasingly to use every situation experienced by humankind as a means to lead them to the path of unbelief. For example, poverty causes people to frequently regret and despair of the situation that has been destined for them. Slowly but surely, devils whisper evil words, until the feelings of regret and despair eventually turn into a denial of the divine justice of Allah, Most High. They may plant deep-seated feelings of hatred and enmity, which result in conflict among people leading to murder. They also delude people with false hopes and dreams, to make them so preoccupied with such thoughts until they become lethargic and neglectful of their responsibilities as *Khalifah* (vicegerent) of Allah on earth.

These are various examples of deceit and instigation by devils to cause humankind to fall into the pit of self-humiliation. Each evil and despicable act they perpetrate on this earth becomes the catalyst for other people to share in the dissemination of misguidance and destruction, until they become the inhabitants of Hell alongside Iblis and his followers. In the book, *'Ihya' 'Ulum ad-Din*, Imam Al-Ghazzali compares the hearts of believers to a wall, and the devil as an enemy bent on demolishing it. In order to protect and safeguard the wall from this destructive foe, the believers must close off all roads and other passages leading to it to prevent the Jinn and devils from getting near and taking control of it.

Among the doors and entrances that open the way for Jinn and devils to destroy humankind are the doors of anger and lust, envy and jealousy, greed, love of life, lack of patience, and suspicion of your Muslim brother or sister.

In another similitude, Imam Al-Ghazzali likens the devil to an insatiably hungry dog continually searching for food and the impure human heart as the place to find it. This means that the heart, which is black, will therefore become the place where the devil will set up residence and remain indefinitely.

It will not be sufficient to expel the devil solely by reciting *"Bismillahir-Rahmanir-Rahim"* ("In the name of Allah, Most Compassionate, Most Merciful") or *"A'udhu billahi minash-shaitanir-rajim"* ("I seek Allah's protection from Satan, the accursed"). Unless the person is of those who have a pure heart and preserve their relationship with Allah the Almighty, only this will strengthen and enable them to drive away the Jinn and devils.

In effect, the deceit and cajoling of the devil will have no effect on the person of *Taqwa* (God-consciousness) who possesses a pure heart free from internal or external defilement. Allah says:

"No authority has he (Satan) over those who believe and put their trust in their Lord." (An-Nahl: 99)

Nowadays, performances by illusionists and stage magicians and stories of the supernatural have become a part of the entertainment business and have a considerable effect on society. It would not be extreme to say that these supernatural acts leave those being entertained absolutely fascinated, almost mesmerized. More surprising than the fact that these acts are viewed as entertainment or pastimes is that they are the inspiration for certain individuals to learn the techniques or ways of possessing these extraordinary powers.

Whenever television programs are aired featuring magicians or illusionists, or even certain supernatural stories or horror films, almost all regular viewers are fairly certain or even completely convinced that the contents of these programs are real or actually exist. Moreover, these programs often feature characters that look unusual and possess special powers, such as jumping or flying high, and performing deadly fighting moves to combat mysterious, Jinn-like creatures.

These phenomena, in one way or another, have a serious impact on the perception of viewers, particularly those who are totally obsessed with the supernatural. The most worrying aspect of these phenomena is that they implant an incorrect understanding regarding the true situation of the unseen world. They obscure the boundaries of reality and fantasy. In the long run, these phenomena will become the inspiration for a few who have the desire to study and control supernatural knowledge such as is portrayed.

This is where a dangerous situation becomes more acute. The moment humankind becomes impressed with the skill and extraordinary ability of those who have knowledge of the supernatural, Jinn and devils will begin to inject their poison by whispering into the unconscious mind. This will result in many people going astray from Islam.

In reality, a confused understanding regarding the unseen world cannot solely be blamed on television programs. Fundamentally, human beings themselves possess a very primitive perception regarding the existence of the unseen world and Jinn. For example, in any given society, people will know various amazing or scary stories regarding strange events or happenings that they may have experienced personally.

Throughout the whole world, diverse names or epithets are used for Jinn and devils. Although the names may be different, their mission is one and the same: to spread evil, sow discord, and misguide humankind. All of this to fulfill their responsibility of persuading humankind to be disobedient to Allah the Almighty.

As for the ability of humankind to see Jinn in their true form, the issue is shrouded in confusion and misunderstanding, which is far from the truth. Some people are influenced by allegedly true stories of those who claim to have met Jinn in their original form, those who have unintentionally caught Jinn on film in their real shape, or various other issues in connection with the true identity of Jinn.

Regarding these issues, Allah has decreed:

"...for he (Satan) and his tribe see you from a position where ye cannot see them..."
(Al-A'raf: 27)

This verse clearly shows us that the same eyes we use to see and experience life in this world do not have the capability to look at Jinn or devils in their original form. We can only see them when they appear in a different form. On this basis,

Ibn Hajar said, "Satan has the ability to appear in forms that we are able to see."

Generally, there is a confused notion that Jinn and devils fear the sun and avoid its rays. This idea is portrayed, for example, in Dracula films or stories of vampires.

This myth is perpetuated by such stories in scenes where the vampire is in a state of extreme terror at the rising of the sun. Fear of sunlight causes them to rise only at night to search for victims. In fact, Jinn and devils are always active at any time or place, day or night.

In addition to this, there is the mistaken general belief that those who died under unusual circumstances, such as torture or murder, will rise up and haunt the earth in a tormented state. Other stories further add that these prowling spirits are seeking revenge or cannot rest until they complete unfinished business.

The true state of affairs, however, is that whether these spirits were good or evil, the moment they were separated from their bodies, they were brought to a place determined by Allah the Almighty. The spirits of pious people have a different place from that of the spirits of unbelievers.

In Islam, the concept of ghosts, i.e. spirits of the dead who haunt the earth, does not exist. These shadows of people who have passed away possess no connection at all with rising from the grave and haunting the earth. These phenomena fall under two possibilities. Firstly, they may just be figments of people's imagination or hallucinations. Or secondly, they may be a result of Jinn appearing in human form.

One of the characteristics of the Jinn is the power to change themselves into different forms. This power, of course, is by the permission of Allah the Almighty. The only form that Jinn and devils cannot impersonate is the Prophet Muhammad. This was confirmed by him in the collections of Hadith by Imam Al-Bukhari and Imam Muslim.

In short, the only way taught by Islam to prevent interference from the Jinn and devils in our lives, or even from the evil of humankind, is by surrender to Allah and placing total reliance on Him. It is imperative always to read, practice and live by all that is contained in the Qur'an every day in our lives.

The Prophet Muhammad said, "Satan flees from the house in which Surah Al-Baqarah is read" (Hadith narrated by Muslim). Quranic verses and du'as to Allah are the only way to protect oneself and fend off assaults by Jinn and devils, as well as the evil that springs from the intentions of humankind.

This, so far, is more or less the general picture of questions and issues of phenomena that shroud human perception regarding the world of Jinn. Whatever the case, only Allah the Almighty is All-Knowing about the true situation of their world. Allah knows best.

DU'A

O Allah! You are my Lord. There is no God except You. You created me and I am Your slave. I am ready to fulfill my promise to You according to my full capability. I seek Your protection from the evil I have done.

I am grateful for Your blessings upon me. I turn to You, as a sinner. My Lord! Forgive me. There is no one who can forgive sins except You.

CHAPTER 1: THE WORLD OF JINN FROM THE ISLAMIC PERSPECTIVE

Humankind uses various terms to describe supernatural beings, such as "ghost," "ghoul," "phantom," etc. In the Qur'an, they are referred to solely as devils or Jinn. These names and terminologies used by people to illustrate various forms of demonic manifestation do not represent different species or beings possessing individual existences. In reality, they are all Jinn or devils appearing in different forms.

The Qur'an clearly points out that all Jinn, like humankind, bear the duty and responsibility to fulfill Allah's commands and prohibitions. The Jinn consist of those who are good and obedient (Muslim Jinn), and those who are evil and rebellious. Evil Jinn are classed as devils.

Within the branch of Islamic teachings pertaining to the ways and characteristics of the Jinn, the origins of their creation are mentioned. Whereas humankind was created from a sperm-drop, Jinn were created from flaming fire. Allah the Almighty has also bestowed on them longevity, as is deduced from the vow of Iblis (Satan) to misguide the progeny of Prophet Adam until the Day of Judgment.

Allah has given Jinn and devils the power to change shape and travel vast distances at considerable speed. These feats are within the capability of both Muslim and non-Muslim Jinn, but only by the knowledge and permission of Allah the Almighty.

Numerous Hadith of the Prophet mention those among his companions who came across Jinn in various forms such as snakes, dogs, or humans dressed in black or white robes, as well as another apparitions.

The main objective of the Jinn and devils' mission on this earth is to spread evil in order to misguide humankind, causing them to become the inhabitants of Hell. In the Qur'an, the words of Iblis are narrated:

"O my Lord! Because Thou hast put me in the wrong, I will make (wrong) fair-seeming to them on the earth, and I will put them all in the wrong, except Thy chosen servants among them."
(Al-Hijr: 39-40)

It is explained in Surah Al-Jinn in the Qur'an that the Jinn generally fall into two categories. The first are those who obey Allah's commands and prohibitions. The second are those who deviate from the truth and spread evil on the earth:

"**Amongst us are some that submit their wills (to Allah) and some that swerve from justice. Now those who submit their wills, they have sought out (the path) of right conduct: but those who swerve, they are (but) fuel for Hell-fire.**"
(Al-Jinn: 14-15)

The Prophet said: "O Abu Dharr, did you seek Allah's protection from the evils of Jinn and mankind?" (Hadith narrated by Ahmad.) This Hadith is further strengthened by the following Quranic verse:

"**Likewise did We make for every Messenger an enemy; devils among men and Jinn...**"
(Al-An'am:112)

This verse provides clear proof that that there are two types of devils: Jinn and human. Human devils are people who are dominated by Satan and their own passions and desires to the point where their natures are not very different from Jinn devils who are continually misguiding and persuading humankind to perpetuate all kinds of evil and destruction. The term 'devil,' therefore, can also refer to evil human beings.

Befriending and forging ties with Jinn

The concept of humankind befriending Jinn is not something easily understood by all people. Even though Jinn and humans occupy different dimensions, there is room between these two worlds for them to form relationships.

Muslim scholars are unanimous that friendship with non-Muslim Jinn is forbidden. This poses the necessary question: is it permitted to form ties with Muslim Jinn?

On this issue, the scholars are of two opinions. The first opinion allows humans to form such ties, under the condition that the person does not enslave himself to the Muslim Jinn. The second opinion completely forbids any form of relationship with any type of Jinn.

They contend that the worlds of Jinn and humankind are different. The abilities of humans are extremely weak when compared to those possessed by Jinn. It is feared that in such a situation, the human will be dragged down little by little into the pit of deviation from Islam and *shirk* (polytheism). *Na'uthu billahi min dhalik* (We seek refuge in Allah from that).

Prophet Muhammad gave constant reminders to his companions in particular, and to the Muslim *ummah* (nation) in general, to put their full trust in Allah the Almighty. He continually enjoined them to increase their acts of *'ibadah* (worship) to Allah, whatever the situation or problem, in order to keep themselves far away from *shirk*.

Yet for those who have made their lives dependant on the assistance of Jinn, it is not improbable that their trust and dependence on Allah the Almighty will eventually disappear and be replaced with the dependence on the supernatural power of Jinn and devils.

The majority of Muslim scholars agree that the best of Muslim Jinn are equal to the lowest level of *mu'minin* (believers) among humankind. Therefore, it is most unfitting for humankind to ask help from the Jinn, who are of a much lower status than them.

The Prophet himself never once used or asked for help from unseen beings when facing difficulties from the unbelievers of his tribe, the

Quraish, in carrying out his mission of *da'wah* (inviting to Islam). On the contrary, Allah the Almighty commanded the Angels to assist him as a *mu'jizah* (prophetic miracle) and proof of his prophet-hood.

In the Qur'an, there are several verses describing the dialogue between Allah the Almighty and Satan, the personification of rebellion and insolence to Allah, Most Powerful:

(Allah) said: "O Iblis! What prevents thee from prostrating thyself to one whom I have created with My hands? Art thou haughty? Or art thou one of the high (and mighty) ones?"

Iblis said: "I am better than he: Thou createdst me from fire, and him Thou createdst from clay."

(Allah) said: "Then get thee out from here: for thou art rejected, accursed. And My curse shall be on thee till the Day of Judgment."

(Iblis) said: "O my Lord! Give me then respite till the Day the (dead) are raised."

(Allah) said: "Respite then is granted thee— till the Day of the Time Appointed."

(Iblis) said: "Then, by Thy power, I will lead them astray. Except Thy servants amongst them, sincere and purified (by Thy grace)."
(Saad: 75-83)

The existence of Jinn is a fact that cannot be denied. The weight of phenomena discovered and experienced by humankind clearly indicates that these supernatural beings do indeed exist.

In the first three verses of the second chapter of the Qur'an, Allah states:

Alif Laam Miim. This is the Book, in it is guidance sure, without doubt, to those who fear Allah; who believe in the Unseen, are steadfast in prayer, and spend out of what we have provided for them."
(Al-Baqarah: 1-3)

One of the phenomena undergone by certain people is that of being possessed by Jinn or devils. If it occurs only to the level of delirium or nightmares, then almost all of these incidents may be explained from the view of psychology or even physiology. If, however, it occurs to the level where the possessed individual suddenly attains extraordinary physical strength, speaks about something of which he had no prior knowledge, or his whole character and manner changes unexpectedly into someone almost unknown to those around him, then this situation has some form of connection to the Unseen. This type of phenomenon is very difficult for the human mind to comprehend or accept.

Creation of humankind and Jinn

"I have only created Jinn and men, that they may serve Me."
(Adh-Dhariyat: 56)

Allah the Almighty is the Creator of everything that exists in all worlds, whether they exist in the visible world or the invisible world. Allah has also decreed differences in the creation of Jinn and humankind; Jinn were created from flaming fire and humankind from dry clay.

Allah the Almighty, in several places in the Qur'an, clearly states about the origins of Jinn from flaming fire:

"And the Jinn race, We had created before, from the fire of a scorching wind."
(Al-Hijr: 27)

"And He created Jinn from fire free of smoke."
(Ar-Rahman: 15)

(Allah) said: "O Iblis! What prevents thee from prostrating thyself to one whom I have created with My hands? Art thou haughty? Or art thou one of the high (and mighty) ones?"

Iblis said: "I am better than he: Thou createdst me from fire, and him Thou createdst from clay."
(Saad: 75-76)

The creation of Jinn and devils from flaming fire took place even earlier than the creation of humankind. It is not surprising that the traits of inflicting pain and cruelty, coupled with an evil and despicable nature that is synonymous with Jinn and devils, bear a connection with their origins from the element of fire. In the same manner, their traits of being deceitful, arrogant, and proud can be compared to the blazing flame that seeks to destroy everything that comes into contact with it.

Origins of the Jinn's creation

Allah the Almighty created the Jinn earlier in time than humankind. The time period between each individual creation of the two beings was very long by human or Jinn estimation. Allah the Almighty states:

> **"And We created man from sounding clay; from mud moulded into shape; and the Jinn race, We had created before, from the fire of a scorching wind."**
> (Al-Hijr: 26-27)

Also in the Qur'an:

> **"...Thou didst create me (Iblis) from fire, and him (Adam) from clay."**
> (Al-A'raf: 12)

> **"And He created Jinn from fire free of smoke."**
> (Ar-Rahman: 15)

Imam Muslim in his *Sahih* collection, notes a Hadith received from 'Urwah, from A'ishah, which narrates that the Prophet said: "Angels were created from light, Jinn from flaming fire, and Adam from that which has already been mentioned to you all."

From examples in the Qur'an and Sunnah, it is clearly evident to us that Jinn were originally created from fire.

Although the human body was, in essence, created from clay, it does not dissolve if it comes into contact with water. The "clay" constitutes a part of its original composition.

Likewise, the same situation applies to the Jinn. They no longer exist in their original form of fire, which may be extinguished by water. They have been moulded by Allah the Almighty into a different form that still constitutes its original composition, i.e., fire, which thereafter was developed and given a shape and functioning organs. Following this, a spirit was breathed into it so that it would become an intelligent, rational being possessing free will. In the same manner, Allah the Almighty created Prophet Adam from clay, known in Arabic as *at-tin*.

By the will and power of Allah the Almighty, the flaming fire became an organism containing fluid-based and non-fluid-based functions. After a spirit was breathed into it, it became a form possessing characteristics and a light and supple body.

In the Holy Book of Islam, Allah the Almighty has informed humankind that the evil Jinn and devils are their bitterest enemy. This enmity will continue until the Day of Judgment. Since the creation of humankind, Allah the Almighty first warned Prophet Adam and his wife Hawwa (Eve) to be continually alert and on their guard from the evil and destruction caused by Iblis and his forces of devils and Jinn.

Although Satan and his progeny are a clear enemy to Adam and the whole of humankind, it must be remembered that Allah the Almighty will, at all times, give guidance and direction to whoever desires it and continually strives to seek it.

Physical appearance of Jinn

In the creation of Jinn and humankind are signs of the perfection and all-embracing knowledge of the Creator of all. Allah the Almighty created Jinn in the same way He created humankind. Although there are differences from several aspects, nevertheless there are still similarities between the two species.

For example, the size of a Jinn's head is larger in proportion to the size of its body. Its eyes are long and not round like human eyes. Some have eyes that arch upwards, while others have eyes in line with the forehead. In general, they possess large, long, and wide eyes, like those of a deer.

In general, there are many misconceptions and mistaken beliefs regarding the appearance of Jinn. They are imagined to possess eyes that are flaming red in color. In fact, they may have black, yellow, or dark-brown eyes; those of black eyes may contain hues of white. The shape of their ears is pointed, like those of a cat.

Jinn possess noses that are situated in the center of their faces, like humans. They may be of various shapes; some are flat, others are round.

Whereas Jinn possess very thick hair, female Jinn have even thicker, lusher hair. The hair of male Jinn is coarser, but many Jinn are bald. The hair of female Jinn is very long, and some keep it so long that it drags on the ground. This is because among them long hair is a sign of beauty.

Jinn possess hands and feet similar to those of humans, but they differ in terms of size. Their hands are longer in proportion to the size of their bodies. Their feet are precisely like the feet of humans, except the angle of the heel and their toes are more pointed.

Generally, there are many confused perceptions about the lifestyle of Jinn. One area that is surprising to most is their style of clothing.

It is not usually known that Jinn wear clothes of various designs that are strikingly beautiful. Female Jinn normally wear clothes that are particular to women or are feminine. Muslim female Jinn wear *hijab* (head veil) or *jilbab* (full-body gown) like Muslim women. Muslim male Jinn wear clothes in the shape of shirts. The majority of Jinn like the colors red, yellow, and black.

Life of Jinn

In the world unseen by human eyes, the population of its inhabitants is far greater than that of people inhabiting this planet. The population of Jinn is quite uncountable. Even though the population of earth is estimated to be over five billion, the exact number is quite unknown. The situation of Jinn is even more extreme, because their numbers go into countless billions.

It is not surprising that the number of Jinn far exceed the number of humans on earth, because Jinn occupy almost all space on the face of the earth on land, air, and sea. As with humankind, Jinn are divided into various different types and races.

Basically, the world of Jinn is not too different from the human world; they are divided into countries, governments, nationalities, tribes, leaders, and the masses. They also follow the various religions practiced by humankind.

As for the difference between devils and Jinn, all devils are Jinn but not all Jinn are devils. Based on Quranic evidence we know that Iblis is from the Jinn:

> **Behold! We said to the angels, "Prostrate to Adam": they prostrated except Iblis. He was one of the Jinn, and he broke the command of his Lord..."**
> (Al-Kahf: 50)

Devils originate from the marriage-like union of Iblis with his followers from the female Jinn.

The progeny born of such unions are called devils or demons.

Iblis himself is not very different from other Jinn. The only difference between devils (Jinn that follow Iblis) and Jinn is that devils have been cursed by Allah the Almighty till the Day of Judgment. Although their progeny have been created with hideous and evil-looking appearances, they still possess the power to appear in any form.

Their physical anatomy includes a very short tail of approximately 4–6 cm or longer, which is only found on devils. Their height falls approximately between 140–160 cm. Exclusive to Iblis is a residence resembling an extremely large palace where he is looked after by millions of helpers and guards.

As previously mentioned, Jinn have the capability for sexual reproduction to perpetuate their race, in the same way as humankind.

Fundamentally, the process of sexual union between male and female Jinn takes place in the same manner as human sexual intercourse, but complementing the smaller size of their physique. Male Jinn will also experience orgasm, produce sperm, feel passion, and possess libido for sexual intercourse, in addition to the same feelings and emotions experienced by human beings.

In the world of Jinn, the age where they are considered mature enough to marry and start a family is generally between 170–250 years old. This is followed by pregnancy and birth. Whereas the time period of human pregnancy is nine months, Jinn pregnancy usually takes fifteen months.

Although human woman experience hardships and problems during pregnancy, the situation is worse for female Jinn. The fifteen-month gestation period begins with the cessation of menstruation. This is accompanied by sensations of pain, because in a single pregnancy Jinn may carry between 7–9 babies. It is not impossible for them to carry 12 babies in a single gestation.

Newborn Jinn infants are very much the same as their human counterparts, in that they pass through the first stage of life lying down without being able to move about or talk, and sleeping for long periods of time.

In a Hadith, the Prophet Muhammad is purported to have said:

"When a man has sex with his wife without mentioning Allah's name (first), the Jinn gather and take part in the sexual act alongside him."

Our lives are at constant risk to the interference and evil of devils and Jinn whose very aim is ruin our day-to-day activities.

Jinn are continually looking for the opportunity to forcibly involve themselves in the intimate relations between married couples. The most worrying aspect of this invasion of privacy when Jinn interfere in the union of husband and wife is not just that they are taking part in the act, but that they may ejaculate their sperm at the same time as the man ejaculates so that it defiles the issue that may be born. Much more alarming is the situation of those who have no link with Allah the Almighty and never pray to Him for His protection. Ever-searching for ways to take advantage of human weakness, it is not impossible for a devil or Jinn to deceive a woman by appearing in the form of her husband and having sex with her. She may then become pregnant from the Jinn's sperm.

Types of Jinn

Prophet Muhammad said: "Jinn are divided into three groups. The first possess wings that allow them to fly in the air. The second are in the form of snakes and dogs. The third have the ability to change from one group to another" (Hadith of an authentic chain of narration from Al-Baihaqi).

In the Qur'an:

"Likewise did We make for every Messenger an enemy; devils among men and Jinn, inspiring each other with flowery discourses by way of deception. If thy Lord had so willed, they would not have done it: so leave them and what they forge."
(Al-An'am: 112)

Whenever the word "devil" is mentioned, it brings to mind a character that is evil, arrogant, proud, despicable, mean, and many other characteristics that people find truly detestable.

Jinn who possess the traits of pride and love of evil are devils. People who possess these same traits are usually deemed as having a devilish character. Animals too may be deemed the same if they are savage, wild, and aim to inflict pain. The Prophet of Allah stated that a black dog is the devil.

If we look at the character of devils besides those that come from the Jinn, there are also those from humankind. This type of character continually influences other people to commit evil, while himself perpetuating all kinds of wickedness and disobedience to Allah. They are the enemy of humankind who deceive them with flowery, soft speech. This speech, however, is poisonous, and its charming, beautiful words are designed to misguide and impel humankind to perpetuate ever more evil and disgraceful acts in the world.

Human understanding of devils and Jinn is, in fact, based on information about them recorded in God's divine revelation sent down to humankind. He alone is All-Knowing and truly understands everything about them. Despite this, there is a significant proportion of humankind who refuses to believe in the existence of unseen beings. These people base their understanding on their own superficial knowledge and groundless opinions. In denying the existence of these supernatural beings, they demonstrate their own lack of open-mindedness.

The position taken by those individuals who deny the existence of Jinn, based on lack of knowledge and observation, does not alter the fact of their actual existence. Any assumed knowledge of such individuals does not particularly qualify them to know about all forms of life in this universe.

Nevertheless, we can be sure that the life-forms that are found in this world may or may not be found on other planets or galaxies. This is a fact that cannot be denied. There is even the possibility that there are other life-forms that occupy alternative dimensions to our own world that have remained undiscovered or unresearched through human learning.

Jinn and devils were created from flaming embers of fire. In addition to this, Allah the Almighty created them with the ability to adapt to living on or outside of the earth. Unlike human beings, they are not faced with difficulties in traveling from one place to another, because they were created with the ability to move very much faster than human beings.

In the same way that there are human beings who are pious and others irreligious, the same applies to the world of Jinn. Among them are those who truly believe and others who are persistently disobedient to Allah the Almighty.

Jinn and all unseen beings occupy the same world as humankind, but what differentiates them from humans is solely their dimension, i.e., the unseen world that is hidden from the naked eye. They can see humans, but humans cannot view them in their original form, although humans may sense their presence. In the Hereafter, this special situation will be reversed. They will no longer be able to see humankind there, but humankind will be able to see them.

Jinn and devils continually mix among and live alongside humankind. As for devils, their sole mission is aimed at whispering evil suggestions to mankind in order to misguide them and drag them down into sin and disobedience to Allah the Almighty. They never cease in taking advantage of any opportunity to mislead humankind, who, at the same time, is not aware nor conscious of these devils.

Despite this, there is a group who are constantly protected from the crooked suggestions and whisperings of these devils. These are people who do not cease from the remembrance of Allah. They continually beg His protection and strive to bring themselves ever closer to Him. People who always place their full trust in Allah the Almighty and preserve their link with Him through their acts of *'ibadah* (worship) thereby avert devils away from them. Acts of *'ibadah* and *dhikr* (remembrance) of Allah the Almighty become the believers' protective shield against the trickery and interference of devils and Jinn, who are completely weak when up against the Greatness of Allah, Most Powerful.

Taken from another aspect, Jinn and all of the inhabitants of the unseen world, in reality, will follow the same destiny that has also been fixed for mankind. They too, at a determined time, will be brought to account for the good and bad deeds they did. Following this, Allah the Almighty will reward those among His slaves who did good and believed with Heaven. On the other hand, an extremely painful punishment awaits those counted among the group of Iblis, who did evil and disobeyed Allah the Almighty, in the fire of Hell.

Among Allah's creation in the unseen world hidden from human eyes, Jinn are, in fact, weaker and powerless when compared to Allah's Angels.

"Likewise did We make for every Messenger an enemy; devils among men and Jinn, inspiring each other with flowery discourses by way of deception. If thy Lord had so willed, they would not have done it: so leave them and what they forge."
(Al-An'am: 112)

The above verse clearly shows that those who harbor enmity to the Prophets and cause suffering to their followers are devils. These are devils from humankind and, in addition to the devils from the Jinn, they both play a role in misguiding humankind and obliterating goodness from this world. Fundamentally, they take upon themselves the same objective, although they inhabit different dimensions.

Devils and Jinn are in a cripplingly weak position when up against people who continually hope for the pleasure and protection of Allah. Let alone to misguide them, it is extremely difficult for devils and Jinn to come close to Allah's believing and pious slaves. Allah the Almighty constantly protects and safeguards the faithful from interference and evil. Although Jinn and devils possess power and ability above and beyond humankind, despite these advantages they are still very weak when faced with the aid and assistance given by Allah to His pious slaves who are obedient to His commands and avoid all that He has forbidden.

Allah the Almighty has given Satan permission to carry out this work to misguide humankind until the Day of Judgment. By this, humans are tested in order to make them aware that they will be included either among those who are blessed by Allah or cursed by Him. Through the disturbance and evil of Jinn and devils, Allah the Almighty intends to purify and cleanse their hearts, as well as test their patience, in relation to the trust and responsibility given to them as His believing slaves.

If humankind possesses the ability to go through these tests and trials with strength and perseverance, Allah will remove these trials from them and in effect, render all Jinn and devils ineffective against them.

There is a hidden wisdom behind the permission given by Allah the Almighty to Jinn and devils in spreading deceit and evil on earth. Humankind must be patient and unyielding at the moment when evil and ignominy surround them, and they must show the level of their sincerity in discharging their duties and responsibilities as His slaves.

The more that people strive to live by the guidance and direction sent down to the whole of humankind through Prophet Muhammad, the more that devils—be they from humankind or Jinn—will be unable to trick or drag them down into the pit of sin and dishonor. Devils are totally incapacitated and unable to go beyond the limits that Allah has decreed for them.

Those who guard their piety and faith in Allah will surely be aware that their Lord has given these chances to Jinn and devils only as a test and trial for humankind. Even though they possess gifts and abilities far beyond the reach of humankind, in reality they are totally weak and powerless against the mercy and protection of Allah for those of humankind who keep a good relationship with Him as His believing, pious slaves.

This whole situation is according to Allah's will and consistent with that which He has decreed. Whatever outcome takes place at the end of life in this world for every person and whatever was done to them by Jinn and devils, it should be learned that the hidden meaning behind all of this was solely to purify and cleanse them as Allah's servants. Humankind should constantly be aware that the fleeting life of this world will become much better by rejecting the deceitful advances of devils.

By the love of goodness and patience, humankind will certainly receive the mercy and pleasure of God that has already been promised. As for the evil and destruction carried out by devils and Jinn in striving to misguide humankind on this earth, the result is sin and eternal punishment in the fire of Hell. All of this gives immeasurable value and meaning as examples and lessons to prevent our straying into the path of misguidance.

Stories and clear facts from the verses of the Qur'an graphically illustrate an endless war and eternal enmity between devils from humans and Jinn and humankind since the time of Prophet Adam. These same verses do not neglect to give instruction and direction to humankind that the only path to resist these foes is to hold fast to God's guidance and unceasingly pray for His protection. This situation also makes clear that the life of humankind in this world will be continually surrounded by all different elements of evil and ignominy, which are united in their aim to misguide and annihilate humankind.

Characteristics of Jinn

Evil Jinn and devils truly enjoy and derive pleasure from seeing people who are constantly negligent in the remembrance of Allah the Almighty. They continually desire to keep very close to such people in order to control and influence them until their lives end in wickedness and rebellion to Allah the Almighty.

Nevertheless, devils and Jinn simultaneously struggle hard to get closer little by little to people who believe and strive to bring themselves ever closer to Allah the Almighty. Devils and Jinn never stop trying to disrupt their thoughts or psyche, confuse them, or put obstacles in their paths in order to prevent these individuals from becoming aware or recognizing that they may be approaching the path of misguidance.

Devils and Jinn truly love, as well, to whisper suggestions that may cause humankind to lose their grip and strength in remaining firm on the path of goodness and truth. This particularly applies to people who strive to perform the obligations of religion.

As humankind is unable to see or even sense their presence clearly, they are always exposed to the trickery of devils and Jinn. They are totally unaware that at the moment the devils and Jinn inject their poison in order to influence them, they may be in the middle of reflecting and questioning themselves as to the right or wrong of the acts or deeds the Jinn and devils have suggested to them. In this manner many people are tricked and deceived, because at that moment of reflection or self-analysis, they are actually talking to the devils and Jinn who have entered inside them.

Devils and Jinn strive hard so that humankind is preoccupied with numerous day-to-day affairs, and all kinds of problems, desires, and dreams. Devils will take advantage of the desires of human nature by whispering evil suggestions, until their original good intention in carrying out their worldly responsibilities changes and becomes evil and calamitous for them.

Devils struggle hard so that people do not think about the question of abstaining from Allah's prohibitions and avoiding things forbidden while performing their responsibilities and fulfilling the wants and needs of human nature, such as attaining wealth and countless other desires and dreams. They will whisper their evil suggestions until humankind reaches the point where they think that nothing is *haram* (forbidden) and there are no longer any limits or prohibitions to attaining all they desire.

In every good act that humankind intends, Jinn are looking for every opportunity to exploit the Beautiful Names and Greatness of Allah the Almighty. They focus on Allah's characteristics of Most-Merciful, Most-Compassionate and Oft-Forgiving, until in the eyes of humankind already caught in their trap, they no longer see any limits or prohibitions. Eventually, they will feel sure that whatever they do on this earth is for good and with pure intention, and even with full conviction that it is in the name of truth.

While spreading wickedness on the earth, devils and Jinn will also never tire in attempting to render human fear regarding Allah's punishments and retribution as ineffective and unable to prevent humankind from doing evil. Those lost human beings who have already imbibed these perverted ideas and suggestions of Satan will always be convinced that they are on the correct path as long as they believe in Allah the Almighty.

As a result of all these satanic ideas and suggestions, the devils and evil Jinn will bring them to the conclusion that as Allah the Almighty is Oft-Forgiving and Most-Merciful, they are free to do whatever they please because, in the end, Allah the Almighty is surely going to be merciful and forgive them, for they believe that Allah the Almighty is Oft-Forgiving of their sins.

Devils and Jinn are true experts in creating chaos and anarchy in the world. They are "planners of evil" who are adept in formulating strategies and steps to create destruction among everything on earth, particularly humankind.

They may be compared to experts in psychology, who study all facets of human emotion and mental states. Armed with their knowledge, it is easy for them to persuade, convince and recruit humankind to join their "Party of Evil" across the globe.

Satan has never ceased in his efforts to convince humankind that whatever sin or evil they commit may be rationalized in the name of goodness and truth. Eventually, humankind becomes confused and hypnotized by all types of evil and immorality that has been made acceptable before their very eyes through this satanic rationalization. As a result, people deluded in this way will believe that this world has been created with countless pleasures and delights that must be enjoyed to the fullest. In this manner, devils and Jinn formulate their psychological strategies to destroy humankind's success in the Hereafter.

The tribe of Iblis

"O ye Children of Adam! Let not Satan seduce you, in the same manner as he got your parents out of the Garden, stripping them of their raiment, to expose their shame: for he and his tribe see you from a position where ye cannot see them: We made the devils friends (only) to those without Faith."
(Al-A'raf: 27)

The above-mentioned verse shows us a certain reality behind the creation of devils. Jinn are the twin of devils, who like them, were created from flaming fire. This is one of the reasons why it is not easy to see devils in their original form. Even if humans should see them, it would be due to them changing from one form to another, or from one place to another.

The places they truly desire to be in are those where Allah's name is never mentioned. These are places where not even the weakest example may found of people aware of their role as a responsible slave of Allah, fulfilling their duty as His *khalifah* (vicegerent) on earth; to spread goodness and truth and make them flourish throughout the earth.

Allah the Almighty has commanded humans to live their lives consistently with the demands of shouldering the responsibility to advance goodness and truth in the world. Allah the Almighty has also reminded humankind to battle against the falsehood and evil disseminated by devils and Jinn. This will result in humankind being able to build a life resplendent with His pleasure and mercy in this world and tomorrow in the Hereafter.

Muslim Jinn

"Behold, We turned towards thee a company of Jinn (quietly) listening to the Qur'an: when they stood in the presence thereof, they said, 'Listen in silence!' When the (reading) was finished, they return to their people, to warn them.

"They said, 'O our people! We have heard a Book revealed after Moses, confirming what came before it: it guides to the Truth and to a Straight Path.

"'O our people, hearken to the one who invites (you) to Allah, and believe in Him: He will forgive you your faults, and deliver you from a Chastisement Grievous.

"'If any does not hearken to the one who invites (us) to Allah, he cannot escape in the earth, and no protectors can he have besides Allah: such are in manifest error.'"
(Al-Ahqaf: 29-32)

Jinn are divided into two groups: Muslim Jinn and *kafir* Jinn (devils). The Quranic verse above describes an actual historical event where Allah the Almighty sent a group of Jinn to listen to the recitation of some Quranic verses from the Prophet Muhammad. All the while they were listening to his recitation, the Prophet was not aware of their presence, although he was the most honorable and most special person on the earth. From this point, he personally possessed limited knowledge regarding issues of the Unseen, except that which Allah the Almighty permitted him to know. Following this, it was

Allah who informed him about this important event that taught a highly significant lesson.

After they heard the verses of the Qur'an recited by the Prophet in a beautiful and captivating style, the Jinn present then gave their pledge, which was a manifestation of their acceptance of Muhammad as the Prophet and Messenger sent to all worlds. At the same time, it was a symbol of their recognition of the Qur'an as the sacred True Message of religion.

They returned to their community and families, inviting them to believe in Allah the Almighty as the One God, Muhammad as His Messenger, and the Qur'an as the Message of Truth revealed to him.

Shortly after the event, the members of this group of Jinn each become a true *da'i* (inviter to Islam), delivering the truth that came to the Prophet of Allah within their community and society. They also reminded their society that whatsoever rejects the message of the Qur'an will receive retribution and painful punishment in Hell.

Since that time, the beings of the Unseen world who believe have disseminated their activities of *da'wah* (inviting to Islam) with the aim of spreading goodness and truth, particularly in their world.

It follows that there may be many among us who are naturally curious as to how and in what manner they live by the commands contained in the Qur'an in their day-to-day lives. These commands include, for example, *salat* (prayer), fasting, paying *zakat* (alms) and the various other acts of worship that are fundamental according to the teachings of Islam.

It should be remembered that Allah the Almighty has endowed the Jinn with amazing powers and abilities that are extremely difficult to be understood by the human mind. The same applies if we try to understand how they fulfill the obligations and commands demanded by the faith of Islam. It is sufficient to know and believe that, in the same way as humankind, they fall either among the group who reject the Message of Islam, or the group who believe and acknowledge the Qur'an as the truth and the Word of Allah the Almighty.

Activities of devils

Devils and Jinn are busy engaged in various worldly activities, but particularly in the ruination and destruction of the human nation on earth. They go from place to place on literally thousands of unfinished errands or tasks. All the while they are given the opportunity to misguide the descendants of Prophet Adam. They never cease to be occupied.

The activities they carry out follow various strategies that affect either the physical or mental state. They attack psychologically and give rise to continuous feelings of confusion and doubt. In this manner, they find ample ground to fill human uncertainty with evil and wickedness.

In any place they are found, they fill those people with fear who are uncertain about doing good acts. They continually whisper confusing ideas to deceive them, so that they fall into the trap that ends in a terrible fate in this life and the next. They consider people who possess no true belief in and sincerity to Allah as the easiest group to stray into the path of destruction.

Jinn and devils co-operate with each other to create problems that cause mutual hatred among people, which may result in conflict and open hostility. An atmosphere of hatred and enmity among humankind is the environment truly enjoyed by the devils and Jinn who follow Iblis, cursed by Allah. In creating situations of bedlam, devils really feel at home.

It is ironic that they are never negligent in making humankind ever negligent of Allah the Almighty. They utilize people's daily affairs of this world as a factor and excuse for them to become lax in their responsibilities of worship and obligations to the Lord of all.

They will surreptitiously slip into the hearts and minds of people to assume the role of a "guide" in running their day-to-day affairs. Those caught in their snare of deceit will eventually consider this "guide" of the heart as an instinctive voice that cannot be ignored and a source of justification for indulgence in all kinds of evil and immorality.

Devils and Jinn will, however, attempt to disguise their true identities as whisperers of evil so that humankind will not attempt to avoid or distance themselves from them. The name of "devil" is synonymous with any act of evil and makes those souls who still possess a pure heart turn away from them immediately.

It greatly interests devils and Jinn to sneak into the hearts and minds of humans at a crucial moment—the second they forget Allah the Almighty—in order to inject their deceit and evil suggestions. In this manner, people make the incorrect decision in the choice between right or wrong.

Devils and Jinn have inherited the trait of revenge from Iblis. They, in turn, strive to pass this trait on to humankind. As a result, people will never be forgiving and become full of hatred and ill-expectations of each other.

Devils and Jinn unceasingly manipulate humans, who are unaware that very gradually they begin to glorify and idolize evil and adore actions that oppose Allah's commands. Eventually, they will cause those humans who adore and idolize evil to begin worshipping and believing in them. This follows because obeying the directions and whispers of the devils and Jinn is tantamount to bowing in obedience to all commands and prohibitions of Satan; in effect, becoming his slave.

They will be unceasing in bringing their ambitions to fruition by misguiding humankind, and thereby altering and sealing humankind's share of goodness in this life and the Hereafter. Eventually, all humankind's hopes and future will depend on the commands and teachings of the Jinn and devils.

A shocking aspect of Jinn and devils, which is also viewed with abhorrence by Allah in the Qur'an, is their teaching of magic or witchcraft to humankind. At its very basic level, there is a condition of which those who learn these arts may or may not be aware. They must swear loyalty to and acknowledge a mutual agreement between themselves and the Jinn or devil. In teaching humankind these evil arts that disturb and ruin the tranquility of people's lives, the primary objective of these devils and Jinn is to destroy humankind, whether they are those who learn the evil arts or those who become the victims of their black magic.

They also give news of the Unseen to those persons who become mediums, palm-readers, astrologers, shamans, or soothsayers, but only after these black-arts practitioners have fulfilled specific conditions that were previously stipulated.

Jinn and devils always give encouragement to humankind to carry out actions that go against the norms of human ethics and morals. They urge people to openly embrace these actions until they become a culture or way of life for certain groups of individuals.

They push humankind to perform evil or immoral acts either secretly or openly, with the aim that people will consider without any shadow of a doubt that these acts are lawful.

They truly desire that humankind will feel no shame or embarrassment in sexually immoral sins, until they reach the stage where they are confident and sure enough to perpetuate sexual immorality and evil without guilt or secrecy. Eventually, these evil, sexually-depraved people will believe with full conviction that others who do not take part or join in with them acknowledge their activities are acceptable. They will even proclaim that their rampant evil acts should be followed and respected by others.

The earth is not the exclusive possession of humankind. Everywhere we see other forms of life such as animals and plants—not forgetting other life-forms unseen by the naked eye—all of which inhabit this world, too. Unlike animals and plants who occupy the same dimension as us, however, unseen beings have been given a "homeland" or dimension solely occupied by their own community.

Jinn have no knowledge of the Unseen

"Then, when We decreed (Solomon's) death nothing showed them his death except a little worm of the earth, which kept (slowly) gnawing away at his staff: so when he fell down, the Jinn saw plainly that if they had known the Unseen, they would not have tarried in the humiliating chastisement (of their task)."
(Saba': 14)

In this story, at his time of death Prophet Sulaiman was leaning on his staff. The Jinn under his command, who were carrying out heavy tasks, were unaware of his death, when a small worm started to gnaw away at his staff. The staff was eventually worn away to such an extent that it could not support his weight. His lifeless body then fell to the ground, and at that point the Jinn knew he had passed away. Indeed, the Jinn did not know anything about the Unseen as is clearly mentioned in the Qur'an:

"... the Jinn saw plainly that if they had known the Unseen, they would not have

**tarried in the humiliating chastisement
(of their task)."**
(Saba: 14)

Belief of the Jinn in Allah the Almighty

The Jinn and even devils possess the
inclination and conscience to be able to receive
the truth and to believe in Allah the Almighty.
This is illustrated in the Quranic verse that gives
proof of the Jinn listening to guidance and
expressing their belief to their community:

**"And as for us, since we have listened to
the guidance, we have accepted it: and any
who believes in his Lord has no fear, either
of a short (account) or of any injustice."**
(Al-Jinn: 13)

In the same manner, when people listen to
guidance they are listening to the Qur'an, but
they call the Qur'an "guidance," for its value
and essence is the guidance of Allah. They then
declare their faith in Allah, and this is the faith
of a believer in his Lord.

This is also the faith of one whose heart feels
peace in Allah's divine justice and strength, and
in the reality of *Iman* (belief) in Him. Allah the

Almighty is Just. He does not deprive the rights of believers to the smallest degree, nor does He burden His slaves beyond their limits.

The believer continually feels peace and tranquility in Him. "He does not fear loss of reward, nor increase in sin and mistakes." The feeling of peace generates tranquility and removes depression, so that even in hardship one feels no sorrow. On the contrary, one considers hardship as a test from Allah, which brings reward and the opportunity to make more du'a to Him so that He may remove the hardship.

One of the blessings that Allah the Almighty bestowed on Prophet Sulaiman was a state whose power and control extended into the real and unseen worlds. From the moment he came to power, Prophet Sulaiman did not solely rule men, but also all of Jinn. The citizens under Sulaiman's rule were not just humankind, but also Jinn and even animals, including the Hoopoe (a species of bird). This symbolized the power given by Allah to Prophet Sulaiman in effectively communicating with Jinn and animals to carry out his rule as a Prophet appointed by Allah to govern on earth.

It is narrated in the Qur'an that one day Prophet Sulaiman assembled his forces comprised of men, Jinn, and animals. The Hoopoe bird was not present at the muster. When Prophet Sulaiman summoned him, his excuse was that he had just arrived from the land of Saba' (located in current-day Yemen). The Hoopoe informed him that Saba' is a prosperous country ruled over by a queen called Balqis.

As is well-known, Sulaiman was not just a Prophet, but also and administrator and ruler. The Hoopoe went on to inform him that the queen of Saba' worshipped the sun and not Allah the Almighty. It would not be extreme to say that Allah's Prophet, Sulaiman, was a leader governing the whole world, so he commanded that the queen must give up sun-worship and instead believe and worship Allah alone.

In a letter, Prophet Sulaiman commanded Queen Balqis to accept the true faith of belief in One God. Queen Balqis did not accept but sent her messengers laden with gifts to present to Sulaiman. Prophet Sulaiman, in turn, refused to accept the gifts and ordered the messengers to return with them.

His refusal brought rise to a plan to make her come to Prophet Sulaiman. He ordered if there were any among his chiefs who could bring Balqis' throne to his palace. In short, an *'Ifrit* Jinn, for no particular reason, offered himself for the task. Nevertheless, the ability and speed of the *'Ifrit* Jinn in being able to bring the throne was no match compared to a certain learned man there.

A uniquely important lesson may be concluded from this Quranic story concerning contact between humans and Jinn. Although the Jinn was blessed with various abilities and special powers, these abilities could not stand up to the power and abilities of an ordinary man who possessed a very close connection to Allah the Almighty. It was not his individual power or strength that gave this learned man the advantage over the Jinn's ability and special power. It was his special relationship with Allah, and by that he was favored over other humans or even Jinn.

Jinn can enter inside the human body

In a Hadith narrated by Sayyidah Safiyyah bint Huyay, the Prophet of Allah said:

"Satan moves through the body of the children of Adam in the same way as blood flows through it."

It is clear that a devil can travel the human body like electric current flowing through grid cables. Among these types of devils are those who can totally possess the human body, until the victim becomes completely weak and loses consciousness.

One of the main factors why Jinn enter and possess the human body may be due to the despicable nature of the person himself. A Muslim who is neglectful of the remembrance of Allah the Almighty or carries out actions forbidden by religion is openly surrendering himself to any devil for possession.

Another factor may also be due to an unintentional wrong act perpetrated by a person against a Jinn. For example, when someone disposes of boiling water, pouring or throwing it into the open without mentioning Allah's name and thereby causing the death of children of Jinn or devils. The same can occur if a male Jinn falls in love with a human woman whose habit is to be extreme in style of dress or beautification, or a woman who delights in going out to make a wanton show of her beauty.

The Hadith continue: When we reached Allah's Messenger I said: "I have with me my son who is insane whom I have brought for you to pray to Allah for. He said, 'Bring him to me.' So I went to get him from the group of riding animals (among whom I had left him). I took off his traveling clothes and put on good clothes, and took him by the hand back to the Messenger of Allah . He said, 'Bring him closer to me and turn his back to me.' He then grabbed his garment and began to beat him on his back so much so that I saw the whiteness of the Prophet's armpits. While doing so he said, 'Get out, enemy of Allah! Enemy of Allah, get out!' The boy then began to gaze in a healthy manner quite different from his earlier gaze. Allah's Messenger then sat him down directly in front of him, called for some water for him and wiped his face, then he prayed for him. After the Messenger of Allah's prayer there was none in the delegation better than him."

In order to cure a possessed person and drive the Jinn out of their body, it is sometimes necessary to beat them a number of times. In reality, the beating is not aimed at the possessed person but the Jinn who has taken over his body.

When the person has regained his sanity, he will not be aware of being beaten nor feel any pain as a result of it. At the same time, his body will not bear any marks or wounds from the beating.

The only way to drive out or even kill Jinn is by preparing oneself through *Taqwa* and faith in Allah the Almighty. This means to believe and always have hope in His divine help and to be unflinching in following His commands and avoiding His prohibitions.

Devils and Jinn possess an amazing ability to influence and deceive the minds and hearts of humankind. Nevertheless, this ability has not been granted to them through any right or entitlement of theirs to act in this way, but solely due to the permission of Allah the Almighty. This situation is clearly depicted in a verse of the Qur'an, which records the dialog between Allah and Iblis, the leader of all evil Jinn and devils:

"(Iblis) said: 'Then by Thy Power, I will lead them all astray. Except Thy servants

amongst them, sincere and purified (by Thy grace).'"
(Sad: 82-83)

Therefore, the force of Jinn, devils, and Iblis in controlling the world and humankind is only due to the power and greatness of Allah who granted them permission to do so, as was admitted by Iblis himself. Their only obstacles are those people who continually beg Allah's protection and surrender themselves to Him.

We can never know how Satan manages to influence humankind to fall into misfortune. Likewise, we can never decipher the methods and techniques used by him and his minions to deceive humankind until they eventually stray from the correct path.

Another skill Jinn possess is the ability to listen to and understand any language of humankind. This is mentioned in the Qur'an where a group of Jinn heard the Qur'an being recited. They understood the language and absorbed the meaning. Jinn can receive guidance in the same way as they can be led astray:

"Amongst us (Jinn) are some that submit their wills (to Allah), and some that swerve

from justice. Now those who submit their wills—they have sought out (the path) of right conduct: but those who swerve—they are (but) fuel for Hell-fire."
(Al-Jinn: 14-15)

CHAPTER 2: STORIES OF THE JINN IN THE QUR'AN AND BIBLE

When we wish to discuss the world of supernatural beings, particularly Jinn and devils, we are delving into a very broad topic encompassing many various ideas and assumptions that may or may not be correct. In addition to this, among all the stories or narrations regarding this subject, only a handful reflect actual personal experiences from a very small group of individuals, while the rest are baseless. Despite this situation, nobody can deny the existence of these beings or the effect of their presence on humankind.

The examination of stories connected to supernatural beings is a subject regarded as controversial and extremely difficult to prove. Therefore, it is not surprising that fact and fiction pertaining to their mysterious world becomes confused and obscured to the extreme when differentiating between reality and fantasy.

Nevertheless, the true facts about the existence of unseen beings, as well as their traits and characteristics, are referred to prolifically in various religions and beliefs, particularly Islam.

In this chapter, we will be examining in depth several stories and descriptions regarding unseen beings as described in the Qur'an.

The true reality

Without doubt, it is humankind through their own actions who stumble into misguidance and evil by deviating from the path of divine guidance. In the same vein, humankind is continually oblivious in paying no heed to or even deliberately allowing themselves to drift aimlessly into the areas and paths set up as traps by devils to gain control over them. Those members of humankind who possess no contact or link with Allah the Almighty are at grave risk of exposure to the snares of devils and Jinn. In reality, Jinn are truly aware that they are Allah's creatures whose permission gives them respite only until the Day of Judgment. Among the areas and paths they set up as traps are:

- Persistent Suggestions: These are dangerous feelings of doubt that result in the individual being in a permanent state of unease and uncertainty. Eventually, these feelings will blank out and destroy such people's *'aqidah* (faith) and *tauhid* (belief in One God). In accordance with Allah's command, one should always remind oneself about this satanic trap:

"If a suggestion from Satan assails (thy) mind, seek refuge with Allah; for He heareth and knoweth (all things)."
(Al-A'raf: 200)

- Whispers of Satan: These are the way Satan controls people by seriously weakening their functions of reason and awareness. In order to successfully avoid these evil disturbances, Allah states:

"And say: 'O my Lord! I seek refuge with Thee from the suggestions of the satans. And I seek refuge with Thee O my Lord, lest they should come near me.'"
(Al-Mu'minun: 97-98)

- Blowing: Namely pride, boastfulness, and arrogance towards all of Allah's slaves. These human traits very easily stimulate Satan to control an individual. The Prophet in a Hadith narrated by Umm Salamah, always sought refuge in Allah the Almighty from this:

"O Allah! I seek Your protection from the evil of Satan, the accursed, from his whisper, breath and blowing."

- Breath: Namely immoral suggestions or speech that is obscene or disgusting, used by poets to arouse people's sexual desire until it boils over and they are no longer able to control it. This results in more rampant evil and immoral activity on the face of the earth.

- Presence of Jinn or devils: This is the opportunity presented to devils or Jinn to place themselves in habitations where Angels refuse to enter. These include dwellings adorned with pictures, ornaments, or sculptures of living beings, or those that house dogs, alcohol, or un-Islamic celebrations.

- Touch: This is the most dangerous satanic disturbance, such as where a Jinn enters a woman's womb having sexual intercourse with her or where a Jinn enters the stomach or chest of a man. This satanic touch is described in the Qur'an:

"Those who devour usury will not stand except as stands one whom the Satan by his touch hath driven to madness…"
(Al-Baqarah: 275)

- Profiting of Jinn or devils: This situation is described by Allah the Almighty in His Holy Book:

"On the day when He will gather them all together, (and say): 'O ye assembly of Jinn! Much (toll) did ye take of men.' Their friends amongst men will say: 'Our Lord! We made profit from each other: but (alas!) we reached our term—which Thou didst appoint for us.' He will say: 'The Fire be your dwelling-place: you will dwell therein forever, except as Allah willeth. For thy Lord is full of wisdom and knowledge.'"
(Al-An'am: 128)

This situation clearly refers to the acts of those who practice witchcraft and magic, through which they use the presence of Jinn and devils.

Iblis, the tempter of Prophet Adam

Prophet Adam and Hawwa (Eve) were previously blessed with a truly happy life in Heaven. They enjoyed all the blessings of Heaven with a true sense of thankfulness to Allah the Almighty. Sadly, all of this changed in the twinkling of an eye due to the deceitful plan of Iblis. Prophet Adam and Hawwa were totally unaware that their situation in Heaven was constantly being observed by Iblis, who fostered a deep-seated desire for revenge against them.

Iblis had already felt hatred towards Prophet Adam, because he considered Prophet Adam the cause of his banishment from Heaven following his disobedience of Allah's command to prostrate to Adam as a sign of respect.

The happiness and comfort enjoyed by the couple Adam and Hawwa only increased the envy within Iblis. Eventually, his heart resolved to drag Adam down to the pit of sin, so that Allah would banish the couple from Heaven, just as he was.

Within Heaven was an eternal tree, *Khuld*, that Allah the Almighty strictly forbade should be approached or that its fruit should be eaten by

Adam and his wife. Satisfied that he had found a way he could take revenge on Adam and Hawwa, Iblis began to carry out his life-long mission to deceive humankind until the end of time.

Iblis' first step in deception was to lie to Prophet Adam and his wife by saying that only by eating the fruit of the eternal tree, *Khuld*, would they become everlasting in Heaven. Initially, Adam did not believe him, but very gradually he began to be affected by Iblis' suggestions. Iblis' cunning and relentless effort resulted in him successfully tricking the couple into disobeying Allah's command by approaching the eternal tree and, moreover, eating its fruit.

It was indeed an unexpected shock for the both of them when immediately after consuming the forbidden fruit, the clothes covering their bodies disappeared and they were totally naked. At that moment, they both realized that they had been deceived and had fallen into the lure of Satan's trap. Following this, they both cried out:

"They said: 'Our Lord! We have wronged our own souls: if Thou forgive us not and bestow not upon us Thy Mercy, we shall certainly be lost.'"
(Al-A'raf: 23)

Allah the Almighty then ordered them both to seek repentance and ask forgiveness in the manner recorded in the following Quranic verse:

"Then learnt Adam from his Lord certain words and his Lord turned towards him; for He is Oft-Returning, Most Merciful." (Al-Baqarah: 37)

At that fateful moment, Adam and Hawwa were expelled from Heaven and so began their life on earth. Without a shadow of a doubt, Iblis will continue to be the sworn enemy of Prophet Adam's descendants and will not cease in deceiving them until they follow his party—the party of those who will be cursed and punished in the next life. *Na'udhu billahi min dhalik* (we seek refuge in Allah from that).

Among the important lessons that may be obtained from this story, first and foremost is that Iblis and his followers among the Jinn and devils are continually pursuing the destruction of the human race. This desire for revenge will not cease until the Day of Judgment. Iblis and his followers from the Jinn and devils will be relentless in their efforts until the end of time, to misguide humankind so that they follow the path of evil.

Story of Iblis, the rejected

"(Allah) said: 'Then get thee out from here; for thou art rejected, accursed. And the curse shall be on thee till the Day of Judgment.'"
(Al-Hijr: 34-35)

As is generally known, the issue of Iblis' disobedience to Allah the Almighty when ordered to prostrate to Prophet Adam was the first conflict to occur in the relationship between humankind and Jinn. Originally, Iblis was an individual of the Jinn honored due to his knowledge and acts of worship to Allah the Almighty.

The moment Allah commanded all the Angels and other beings in Heaven, including Iblis, to prostrate to Prophet Adam, they all obeyed Allah except Iblis. When Allah the Almighty questioned Iblis as to his refusal in prostrating to Adam, Iblis replied that he was created from fire whereas Adam was created from clay. It was this statement that became the source of arrogance and pride that overtook Iblis, making him feel sure that he was superior to Adam.

Due to his refusal to prostrate to Adam, his rebelliousness, and disobedience, as well as his reluctance to seek the forgiveness and pleasure of Allah the Almighty, Iblis received Allah's curse and condemnation until the Day of Judgment. What is worse still than the moment he was driven out of Heaven and all its blessings is that Iblis will never be given the chance to gain Allah's pleasure. In Surah Saad, the curse of Allah the Almighty on Iblis is clearly described:

> **"(Allah) said: 'Then get thee out from here: for thou art rejected, accursed. And My curse shall be on thee till the Day of Judgment.'"**
> (Saad: 77–78)

Story of the Messenger to the Jinn community

> **"O ye assembly of Jinn and men! Came there not unto you Messengers from amongst you, setting forth unto you My signs, and warning you of the meeting of this Day of yours? They will say: 'We bear witness against ourselves.' It was the life of this world that deceived them. So against themselves will they bear witness that they rejected faith."**
> (Al-An'am: 130)

The message of this verse is clearly meant for both humankind and Jinn. It imports a beneficial lesson that, in the same manner as humankind, Jinn also received the call to truth from Allah's Messengers. It is known that among them are those who believe and carry out the commands and requirements of faith; these are Muslim Jinn. Obversely, there are those who reject and deny the reality of the truth brought to them; these are accursed devils.

At a future point in time, they will receive a sentence of punishment commensurate with their deeds. The same will apply to those among humankind who followed in their tracks.

The Qur'an describes in the above-mentioned verse a particular event where a group of Jinn returned to their home after listening to a recitation of the Qur'an by the Prophet of Allah the Almighty. This narration, describing their speech and actions after hearing the sacred verses, is clear and convincing evidence for the existence of Jinn. It is also sufficient proof of the Jinn being able to listen to the recitation of the Qur'an in Arabic.

Furthermore Jinn, like humankind, are those of Allah's creation who have the ability to choose between faith and unbelief and are free to follow either truth or misguidance.

The world we inhabit contains countless mysteries and secrets that still remain unrevealed. The environment that surrounds us is populated by creatures that are very different and alien to humankind. These are the occupants of the unseen world, which have been granted abilities and advantages above humankind. Very little is known to us about the mystery of their lives, and this state of affairs will continue until the Day of Judgment.

The reality of our lives is that we are on a journey that is long and uncertain and forms only a small part of the changes and events of the world we live in. The knowledge possessed by humankind today compared that of fifty years ago is far more profuse and advanced.

Likewise, the same analogy may be applied to knowledge of the Jinn. In these times, the discussion of the abilities and powers of the Jinn may certainly raise laughter and disbelief in some quarters. In the future, however, there may come a time when Allah the Almighty gives humanity the opportunity to unveil the mysterious world of Jinn and devils. At that time, a similitude of the subject-matter of discussion may be compared to people of a thousand years ago discussing the capability of mankind to invent a rocket to go to the moon!

Whatever is known by humankind can, in fact, only be in accordance with the abilities and limits decreed for them. The whole of human knowledge is unable to go beyond those decreed limits, let alone to understand issues that Allah the Almighty has intended to keep secret.

If we reflect on all our human limits and weaknesses, it should come as no surprise if we are unable to recognize or see with our own eyes the existence of supernatural beings and all the other mysteries of the Unseen. If we possess very little knowledge regarding the mystery of our own creation, then our knowledge is lesser to the extreme regarding all mysteries of the creation of unseen beings.

Moreover, there are still countless mysteries surrounding supernatural beings that Allah the Almighty has not revealed to us. Our knowledge of them is restricted only to their characteristics, their effect on us, and the manner in which they appear.

It would not be amiss to say that we should be thankful to Allah the Almighty for the knowledge and information regarding unseen creatures that He has described to us in His Book. With the guidance He has revealed, humankind need not fall into misguidance and, at the very least, can be aware that the Jinn are His creation who are individually responsible as His slaves for their deeds.

Story of demonic forces

"And to those straying in evil, the Fire will be placed in full view; and it shall be said to them: 'Where are the (gods) ye worshipped besides Allah? Can they help you or help themselves?' Then they will be thrown headlong into the (Fire), they and those straying in evil, and the whole hosts of Iblis together."
(Ash-Shu'ara': 91-95)

Iblis is reputed to be shrewd and skilled. He was created by Allah the Almighty with an above-average perception and possessing amazing abilities. Even though he was rebellious and received the curse of Allah the Almighty until the Day of Resurrection, Allah the Almighty has still allowed him to utilize abilities not possessed by human beings.

Despite his vow to misguide the descendants of Prophet Adam until the day the dead are raised, the circumstances granted to him by Allah the Almighty are actually a manner in which humankind is tested. Through this, the members of humankind are themselves shown in which group they will be classed: either the inhabitants of Heaven or the inhabitants of Hell.

In his scheme of perpetrating evil on the face of the earth, Iblis carefully plans his strategies, correctly organizes himself and executes his movements completely. He accomplishes his goals through trickery and deceit, raising false hopes and giving position and wealth as bait to misguide humankind. After successfully forming groups and followers, Iblis then arranges them like an army who play a role in furthering the fight for evil. His troops consist of humans and Jinn.

Yet on the Day of Judgment when justice will be established, these are the self-same allies who will be casting accusing glances at each other before they are cast into the Hell-fire. These are the members of the same group who were in misguidance and, in turn, misguided others. On that ominous day, they will dispute with each other, blame one another, and finally each one of them will bewail the awful fate that will befall them forever.

On that day, too, they will truly express the desire to be re-created and sent back to the earth for a second chance, with the intention to do good and repent for their previous deeds. Nevertheless, at that time their wish to be given a second chance of life will be in vain. This situation is poignantly described in the Qur'an:

"They will say there in their mutual bickerings: 'By Allah, we were truly in an error manifest, when we held you as equals with the Lord of the worlds; and our seducers were only those who were steeped in guilt. Now, then, we have none to intercede (for us), nor a single intimate friend. Now if we only had a chance of return, we shall truly be of those who believe!' Verily in this is a sign but most of them do not believe. And verily thy Lord is He, the Exalted in Might, Most Merciful."
(Ash-Shu'ara': 96-104)

Story of humankind worshipping Jinn (devils)

"On the Day He will gather them all together, and say to the Angels, 'Was it

**you that these men used to worship?'
They will say, 'Glory to Thee!' Thou
art our protector—not them. Nay, but
they worshipped the Jinn: most of them
believed in them.'"**
(Saba': 40-41)

Jinn and devils struggle unceasingly to mislead
and deceive the human race. It is their heartfelt
desire that humankind takes them as examples
and role models and in turn becomes their
faithful followers in striving for the values of evil
and wickedness in the world. Their dream is to
see evil and immorality run rampant all over the
face of the earth.

More importantly to them is their vision of
controlling the whole world and its inhabitants,
as another aspect of their disobedience to Allah
the Almighty. Yet in addition to this, their grand
objective is to wreak revenge on us because
Prophet Adam, as the father of the humankind,
was the cause of their prince, Iblis, to be driven
out of Heaven.

They order humankind to speak about
things of which they have no knowledge and to
concoct lies and mistruths that they attribute
to the name of Allah the Almighty. They

disseminate abominations and *fitnah* (discord) across the earth in order to implant in a section of humankind the belief in the embodiment of powers other than Allah the Almighty, that God can appear in human form or vice-versa, that God has a son and wife, or various other lies and falsehoods that drive humanity into setting up partners with Allah the Almighty.

It should always be remembered that Satan continually encourages humankind to deny belief in Allah, the Day of Judgment, Angels, the Prophet Muhammad, and all the teachings Allah the Almighty has revealed through His Prophets and Messengers. A significant number of humankind initially deceived and misled by the lying whispers of Jinn and devils will eventually, without any reservations, reject the truth of religion and belief in Allah the Almighty. The final step for this group is to fall headlong into the path of *shirk* (polytheism).

Despite the fact that is in the nature of devils to unceasingly do evil and spread falsehood, on the Day of Judgment, they will struggle to defend themselves. They will refuse to accept any responsibility for the actions of those human beings who fell into their trap. Furthermore, those misguiding devils and Jinn will rebuke and blame those humans who were easily deceived. This situation is depicted in the Qur'an as follows:

"Like Satan when he says to man, 'Disbelieve!': but when (man) disbelieves, Satan says, 'I am free of thee: I do fear Allah, the Lord of the worlds!' The end of both will be that they will go into the Fire, dwelling there forever. Such is the reward of the wrongdoers."
(Al-Hashr: 16–17)

Story of persuasion by devils

"O ye who believe! Follow not Satan's footsteps: if any will follow the footsteps of Satan, he will (but) command what is indecent and wrong: and were it not for the grace and mercy of Allah on you, not one of you would ever have been pure: but Allah doth purify who He pleases. And Allah is One Who hears and knows (all things)."
(An-Nur: 21)

As it is already understood, Jinn and devils are renowned for their cunning ability to deceive human beings, employing strategies and tactics specially designed for their mission to misguide the whole human race. They are highly skilled in influencing the hearts and minds of people.

They never employ direct methods in ordering humankind to carry out evil, because human nature is fundamentally inclined to good. This is achieved through cunning persuasion that disorientates the person, but is attractive and holds their interest. Slowly but surely, the devils inject their poison of evil until human reason cannot benefit from its ability to distinguish between right and wrong and truth from falsehood. The devils and Jinn who follow Iblis are unceasing and untiring in their efforts to make their mission a success, through the whispering of evil suggestions and the rousing of humankind, until they are completely satisfied that humankind is totally behind them on the path of misguidance.

The Qur'an illustrates the actions of Satan in persuading humankind to evil:

"O ye people! Eat of what is on earth, lawful and good, and do not follow the footstep of Satan for he is to you an avowed enemy. For he commands you what is evil

and shameful, and that ye should say of Allah of which ye have no knowledge."
(Al-Baqarah: 168–169)

Story of Jinn as Prophet Sulaiman's troops

"And before Solomon were marshaled his hosts,—of Jinn and men and birds, and they were all kept in order and ranks."
(An-Naml: 17)

This verse describes how Jinn used to serve as troops in the army of Prophet Sulaiman during the time of his governance. Besides Jinn, other troops and civilians under his rule included human beings and birds:

"…and there were Jinn that worked in front of him, by the leave of his Lord, and if any of them turned aside from Our command, We made him taste of the punishment of the Blazing Fire. They worked for him as he desired, (making) arches, images, basons as large as wells, and (cooking) cauldrons fixed (in their places): 'Exercise thanks sons of David, but few of My servants are grateful.'"
(Saba: 12–13)

This is a story from history, forever recorded in the Qur'an. As we have been taught, Allah the Almighty made a group of Jinn subject to Prophet Sulaiman. Although in essence Jinn possess strength far greater than that of mankind, Prophet Sulaiman, by Allah's permission, was able to group them into soldiers and citizens performing duties in obedience to him.

They constructed tall, strong buildings as places of worship, as well as images and massive cooking cauldrons. They even put their amazing abilities to use for Sulaiman by diving for gems in the deep oceans. In reality, however, they obeyed Prophet Sulaiman's commands only by the permission of Allah the Almighty. In that bygone time of his rule, Sulaiman's authority encompassed territory that today is known as Palestine, Lebanon, Syria, and Iraq as far as the River Tigris.

Story of the lie about Allah's connection to the Jinn

"And they have invented a kinship between Him and the Jinn: but the Jinn know (quite well) that they will be brought before Him. Glory to Allah! (He is free) from the things they ascribe (to Him)!"
(As-Saffat: 158–159)

In ancient Arab society, there used to be a prevalent, erroneous belief that the Angels were daughters of Allah, born of female Jinn. It was a truly vicious lie created and attributed to Allah by the pagan Arabs. By speaking about things of which they had no knowledge, they perpetrated one of the greatest forms of misguidance and deviation ever to appear on earth.

Story of Jinn assisting soothsayers

"True, there were persons among mankind who took shelter with persons among the Jinn, but they increased them into further error."
(Al-Jinn: 6)

This verse provides the clearest evidence that since ancient times, particularly the time of Arab *Jahiliyyah* (Days of Ignorance before the Prophet Muhammad), there have been countless groups of soothsayers and shamans who have sought the assistance of Jinn. Even though Jinn possess the power to bring benefit or harm, the verse above explains that Jinn, in fact, only increase people in error and sin. This means that no matter how seemingly great the benefit brought by Jinn to humankind, it is vastly outweighed by the harm.

The moment humankind turns to something other than Allah the Almighty in any of the affairs of their daily lives through seeking the aid and protection of Jinn and devils, this will cause their hearts to be continually assailed by feelings of bewilderment and anxiety. Their hearts will never be at peace, and this will be the price they pay for their actions.

Everything other than Allah the Almighty, every living creature that He has created, will certainly perish at a certain time in the future. Only those who depend solely on patience and the power of Allah the Almighty will be brought to an eternal place abundant in His mercy and forgiveness.

Story of Jinn prevented from ascending the heavens

"And we pried into the (secrets of) heaven; but we found it filled with stern guards and flaming fires. We used, indeed, to sit there in (hidden) stations, to (steal) a hearing; but any who listens now will find a flaming fire watching him in ambush. And we understand not whether ill is intended to those on earth, or whether their Lord

(really) intends to guide them to right conduct."
(Al-Jinn: 8–10)

This verse describes the activities of Jinn who are ever attempting to reach the heavens in order to steal information from hearings among Angels regarding the affairs decreed by Allah the Almighty of all living beings on earth.

Following this, they pass on whatever they may have heard to soothsayers, shamans, and practitioners of black arts, who have all taken the Jinn as companions. These soothsayers, shamans, mediums, and clairvoyants who receive this information, in fact, play a role as "errand boy" to the Jinn, aiding them to continue sowing discord everywhere in accordance with the master plan of Iblis.

It is actually the soothsayers and practitioners of black arts who mix truth with falsehood and then spread it among humankind with the aim of making evil and wickedness dominant on earth.

Among those Jinn who claim to steal a hearing of the divine news pertaining to the affairs of this

world are those who do not succeed. The moment
they attempt to touch the firmament, they find
the ascending path very closely guarded. They
will be pursued by a shaft of flame (meteor) that
will kill any of those who pass that way.

It is clear that issues of the Unseen are Allah's
domain hidden from human understanding.
No one from humankind has ever been privy
to Allah's decrees regarding His slaves on this
planet. If Allah the Almighty should ordain
misfortune for humankind, they would certainly
be at a loss and unable to find a way out. Yet if
Allah the Almighty should ordain goodness for
humankind and bless them with direction and
hidayah (guidance), they would certainly gain
success.

*Story of a reminder and warning regarding
humankind and Jinn*

"Soon shall We settle your affairs, O both
ye worlds! Then which of the favours of
your Lord will ye deny? O ye assembly of
Jinn and men! If it be ye can pass beyond
the zones of the heavens and the earth,
pass ye! Not without authority shall ye be
able to pass! Then which of the favours
of your Lord will ye deny? On you will be

sent (O ye evil ones twain!) a flame of fire (to burn) and a (flash of) molten brass: no defense will ye have. Then which of the favours of your Lord will ye deny?"
(Ar-Rahman: 31–36)

Indeed, it is Allah who is great, strong, all-powerful and able to enforce His will. Allah the Almighty has complete power over His two creations, Jinn and humankind. He alone is ultimate in power to give reminders and warnings to His slaves, in order for them to ponder and recognize their origins and the reason for their creation. In addition to this, they should reflect again and again on the bounties and blessings that Allah the Almighty has bestowed on them.

Everything in this whole universe came into existence with one word of Allah the Almighty, *"'Kun' fayakun"* ("'Be' and it is"). On the other hand, the destruction of the universe will come about with just one blow of the Angel's trumpet, which will signify its last moments.

Jinn and humankind have never been able to escape from Allah's sight. Allah the Almighty sees everything they do throughout their entire lives in this world. At the end of all this, Allah the Almighty has the power to determine the final place of all these beings, either in Heaven or Hell.

Allah the Almighty has also asked the question of humankind and Jinn, **"Then which of the favors of your Lord will ye deny?"** (Surah Ar-Rahman). By this question, it is hoped they will remember, be thankful and reflect upon all of the abundant mercy and blessings He has showered upon them.

In the same Surah, Allah the Almighty puts out the challenge to both His creations of Jinn and humankind to pass beyond the boundaries of the firmaments and earth, **"O ye assembly of Jinn and men! If it be ye can pass beyond the zones of the heavens and the earth, pass ye! Not without authority shall ye be able to pass!"** (55:33). Without doubt, no one has the authority to pass beyond these zones except the One, Most High, who possesses all authority Himself.

Story of Jinn and humankind astray

"On the day when He will gather them all together, (and say): 'O ye assembly of Jinn! Much (toll) did ye take of men.' Their friends amongst men will say: 'Our Lord!

We made profit from each other: but (alas!) we reached our term—which Thou didst appoint for us.' He will say: 'The Fire be your dwelling-place: you will dwell therein forever, except as Allah willeth.' For thy Lord is full of wisdom and knowledge. Thus do We make the wrongdoers turn to each other, because of what they earn."
(Al-An'am: 128–129)

These verses illustrate how devils of humankind and Jinn whisper suggestions to each other consisting of delightful words designed as seductive strategies to misguide others. They mutually cooperate as enemies against people of faith and *taqwa* (God-consciousness) in order to lead them astray. They give each other ideas that they use to cast doubts in the hearts of people who sincerely follow the path of Allah the Almighty.

They strive unfailingly to increase their followers from among the section of humanity that has already been convinced and brainwashed by their surreptitious suggestions. They have gathered together and reinforced those among humankind who submit to their lure and follow in their footsteps:

"...their friends amongst men will say: 'Our Lord! We made profit from each other: but (alas!) we reached our term—which Thou didst appoint for us...'"
(Al-An'am: 128)

Those members of humankind that have been seduced, without reflecting on their own origins, in the end will drift aimlessly, reveling in the pleasures of life. They will become arrogant, follow their own desires, and commit all kinds of sins. Jinn and devils will gain pleasure and ease in seeing humankind astray as a result of their enticement and trickery.

Due to the bond of companionship between Jinn and humankind based on their joint struggle to perpetrate ruin and evil on the face of the earth, Allah the Almighty has made them an association of cronies based on mutual aims and actions. He has also made for them an eternal place of return, full of suffering and painful punishment as a reward from Him.

The conclusion of the verse above also clarifies as to the general form of companionship between devils from humankind and Jinn. Unjust sinners, who set up partners to Allah in any form, will always be unified in opposing truth and guidance from Allah. They are mutual partners in enmity towards each and every Prophet and person of faith. Essentially, they possess the same character that manifests itself in various different guises.

Since time immemorial, the pages of history have witnessed Jinn and men, in association as followers of Iblis, assisting each other in opposing and battling against the existing values of good on earth. As a result of the similarity in their characters and traits, as well as the goal of their mutual association and nefarious work in spreading wickedness, their permanent place of return in the Hereafter will also be similar, i.e., Hell-fire, replete with punishment and suffering.

Seeking protection from Jinn and humankind

> **"Say: I seek refuge with the Lord and Cherisher of mankind, the King (or Ruler) of mankind, the God (or Judge) of mankind, from the mischief of the whisperer (of evil), who withdraws (after his whisper),—who whispers into the hearts of mankind,—among Jinn and among men."**
> (An-Nas: 1-6)

An important and evident conclusion to be drawn from this verse is that refuge and protection from the interference of Jinn and humankind who follow in the footsteps of Satan can only be sought from Allah the Almighty. He alone is the Lord of all humankind. He alone is the King of humankind. He alone is the God of humankind. Therefore He is the sole place of refuge and shelter from the evil produced by Jinn and humans that seduces the heart.

Indeed, He is the God and King of everything that exists in the universe. Through His characteristics of being All-Powerful and All-Protecting, humankind is continually dependant on His mercy and providence, in order to be free of all temptation and trickery used by Jinn and devils to misguide them.

The moment the human psyche notices and is aware of any evil suggestions whispered by Jinn and devils, it is imperative to immediately seek Allah's protection and resist any temptation or gentle persuasion.

Although humankind cannot ascertain the ways and means of demonic trickery, they are able to recognize, judge and distinguish the difference between good and evil. The effect of

Jinn and devils' presence in people's lives is very powerful. Jinn and devils will continually search for ways to infect the human psyche and mind with their evil. If people neglect to seek Allah's protection or pray for guidance and direction in knowing the difference between goodness and harm, then the risk of them being dragged down into the pit of evil becomes infinitely greater.

Resistance and opposition to the temptations and trickery of the devils is, in fact, a great *jihad* (striving) that is obligatory in Islam. An issue only too well-known is the war of the descendants of Prophet Adam against the descendants and followers of Iblis, i.e., Jinn and devils, that has raged on since the beginning of their creation. Satan himself vowed to misguide the whole human race as a result of his arrogance and envy towards Prophet Adam.

Though he was granted Allah's leave until the end of time to carry out his mission to lead astray the progeny of Prophet Adam and cause them all to plunge into the fire of Hell, nevertheless this is, in fact, a wise course of action from Allah the Almighty designed to test humankind. Due to Allah's characteristics of being Most Merciful and Most Compassionate, He will not leave humankind exposed, devoid of help and protection to resist Jinn and devils. Allah the Almighty bestows *iman* (faith in Him) as a defensive fortress in which *du'a* (supplication to Him) and *dhikr* (remembrance of Him) becomes a protective shield.

> Ibn 'Abbas narrates, "The Prophet of Allah (peace be upon him) said, 'Satan resides in the hearts of the children of Adam. If one remembers Allah the Almighty, Satan hides. But if one is neglectful (of remembrance) then Satan tempts him.'"

This situation is an illustration of the hostility between humankind and all those who support evil, whether they be from Jinn and devils, or those who follow them from among humankind themselves.

Allah the Almighty is mighty in power over all His creation. If Allah gave permission to Iblis and his minions from Jinn and humankind to wage war against those people who unfailingly put their full trust in Allah and seek His protection, then Allah the Almighty would, in turn, wage war against the evil ones. Iblis and his followers only have the capability to wage war against those who disregard and are neglectful of Allah's commands and prohibitions. Those who unceasingly remember and surrender themselves to Allah the Almighty, by His permission and mercy, will be safe from the evil and harm of Jinn and devils.

Good and honorable deeds are closely connected to absolute strength and power, i.e., the power of Allah, the Creator of all beings. Conversely, evil and harmful deeds will perish when up against Allah's help and support.

This is an explanation of the true reality pertaining to good and evil that exists in the world. These two forces are always in conflict and this hostility will continue until the Last Day. What is certain is that as long as Allah the Almighty protects and blesses His slaves who unceasingly seek His favor and commit themselves to getting ever closer to Him, there is no other power that will ever be able to ruin and misguide them, by His permission.

Story from the Hadith of Allah's Prophet

1. Iblis' promise to misguide the human race

Ever since the incident where Allah cursed Iblis for his refusal to prostrate to Adam, he has borne a very deep-seated grudge against the whole of Adam's progeny. He has vowed to misguide and make the children of Adam disbelieve in Allah, so that in the future life they will enter Hell alongside him.

In a Hadith of the Prophet, it says, "Satan (the curse of Allah upon him) said to his Lord, 'By Your Glory and Majesty, O Lord, I will be unfailing in misguiding Your slaves and ordering them to commit *kufr* (unbelief) and immorality as long as their spirits remain in their bodies.' Then Allah replied, 'O cursed one! By My Glory and Majesty, I will not cease in forgiving them as long as they desire to remember Me and seek My forgiveness.'"

This was one of Iblis' promises to cause humankind to stray so that they reject Allah through the perpetration of ruin and evil on earth. They that become Satan's friends will be in the Hell-fire.

2. Devils spread slander about those devoted to worship

It was narrated from Ibn 'Abbas that there was an *'abid* (man devoted to worship) from the Children of Israel who lived in seclusion. His only company was Angels, who honored him with visits in the morning and evening.

Allah blessed him with ease by causing a grape vine to grow in the surroundings of his place of worship, so that it would benefit him in meeting his daily needs.

One night while he was engrossed in worship, a beautiful woman came to his place calling to him. "O pious one! In the name of Allah, please let me spend the night at your place of worship, for my home is far away."

Before he could answer, the woman stepped into his place and then gradually began to remove all her clothes until she had nothing on her body. The pious man was shocked, and suddenly exclaimed, "Curse you! Put your clothes back on!" She replied, "You must enjoy yourself with me this night!"

So the pious man questioned his *nafs* (ego), "O *nafs*, what is your opinion?" His *nafs* retorted, "You do not have to fear Allah." The pious man said, "Curse you! Do you desire that all my acts of worship be in vain and that I be punished and forced to wear garments of fire? I am truly fearful of being punished in a Fire that will never be extinguished, with a suffering that will never cease. I am sorely afraid should I incur Allah's anger that I will never attain His pleasure and mercy!"

The desire of his *nafs* continually goaded him on to do *zina* (illicit sex) with this immoral woman. As he was caught between two tense, opposing situations of good and evil, suddenly the pious man stretched out his fingers above the fire in his place until the palms of his hands were burnt. The woman was so startled to see the pious man burn his own hands, she screamed so intensely that she died of shock instantly.

But Satan—never ceasing to stoop to any act of deceit against humankind—used the opportunity to sow discord, in compensation for his failure to tempt the pious man with the woman. Iblis spread the lie that the pious man had done *zina* with the woman and then murdered her.

The slander sown by Satan eventually came to the knowledge of the ruler of the time. As a result of this, the ruler declared that the pious man should be arrested and tied and bound by his feet, hands and neck, in the same manner as an animal. In this era, the punishment meted out by society for the crime of *zina* was for the offender's body to be cut in half.

The moment his execution began to be carried out, he felt such excruciating pain that quite unaware, he cried out. Immediately, Allah the Almighty sent the Angel Jibril to him with the message: "Do not cry out again. You are in My sight. Your suffering has made the Angels who carry the Throne and all the inhabitants of Heavens weep. By My Glory and Majesty, if you cry out again, I will destroy the Heavens and cause the earth to swallow up all its inhabitants."

Ibn 'Abbas continued that Allah returned the spirit of the woman to her body, and she came back to life saying,

"The pious man has been wronged. He did not do *zina* with me, nor did he murder me. I am a witness from My Lord!"

An important message that may be gathered from Ibn 'Abbas' narration is that Iblis and his allies among Jinn and devils are always spying for opportunities to cause humankind to deviate. This status quo will continue till the end of time, as long as the light of goodness still shines on earth.

There are several primary points that may be a guide and example as steps to recognize and guard against the deceit and goading of Jinn and devils:

a. Iblis and Jinn may change form and features at will, as fits the situation in their plans to misguide humankind.
b. Iblis at all times invites one to commit evil, unbelief, and immorality.
c. All trickery and evil perpetrated by Jinn and devils to misinterpret as well as break up the faith of Islam is well within the knowledge of Allah.
d. Those who fight and willingly sacrifice their body and soul to uphold the faith of Allah on the face of the earth will always receive protection from Allah the Almighty, as well as, by His permission, the reward of Paradise in the Hereafter.

Story of how Iblis taught Cain to kill

It would not be considered extreme to say that Iblis (the curse of Allah upon him) is an expert in the dealings of immorality and unbelief. He is the chief schemer of evil and disobedience found on the face of the earth.

He is also responsible for the first ever murder among humankind on earth, when he instructed Qabil (Cain) how to kill Habil (Abel).

Ibn Juraij narrates that at the time Qabil intended to murder Habil, he was puzzled because he did not know how it should be carried out.

As it has been constantly emphasized, Iblis and his following of Jinn and devils never allow any chance to pass by where they do not to whisper evil suggestions and cause humankind to stray. Iblis came to Qabil holding a bird that he placed on a rock. He then took a larger rock with which he hit the bird, killing it cruelly.

This incident was of great interest to Qabil, and he used it as an example on which he could eventually base the murder of Habil. The perpetration of this evil deed demonstrated by Iblis became the first shedding of human blood on earth, which all began through his suggestions and entrapment.

Story of the dialogue between the Prophet and Iblis

It was narrated from Wahab bin Munabbin that Allah commanded Iblis to come before

Prophet Muhammad to answer a number of questions to be put forward by the Prophet himself.

Iblis appeared before the Prophet of Allah in the form of an old man with an unblemished face, holding a staff in his right hand. The Prophet inquired of him, "Who are you?" He replied, "I am Iblis." The Prophet continued, "Why have you come here?" Iblis said, "Allah ordered me to come to you and answer the questions you put to me."

Upon hearing this, the Prophet then enquired, "O Iblis, who are your enemies from my *ummah* (nation)?" Iblis replied, "They are fifteen:

1. You, Muhammad, are my deadliest enemy
2. The just leader
3. The rich man who is humble
4. The honest merchant
5. The *alim* (scholar) who prays with complete submissiveness to Allah
6. The believer who gives good advice
7. The believer who strengthens the bonds of brotherhood
8. The person who repents to Allah and remains true to his repentance

9. The person who is cautious of *haram* (forbidden) things
10. The believer who guards his chastity
11. The believer who gives much in charity
12. The believer who possess a character and conduct that is praiseworthy
13. The believer whose life gives benefit to others
14. The person who is consistent in reading the Qur'an
15. The person who prays at the time of night when other people are fast asleep."

Then the Prophet of Allah went on to ask Iblis, "Who are your companions from my *ummah?*" Iblis answered, "They are ten:

1. The corrupt judge (who does not rule in favor of justice)
2. The person who is proud and arrogant
3. The dishonest merchant
4. The person who drinks alcohol
5. The person who spreads *fitnah* (discord)
6. The person who does good deeds only to be seen by others
7. The person who devours the orphan's property
8. The person who makes light the duty of prayer

9. The person who refuses to give zakat (alms)
10. The person who spends his time engrossed in idle thoughts and dreams

All of these are my brethren and close companions!"

This is indeed a hugely beneficial warning that should be taken as a lesson for humankind. From the above-mentioned dialogue between the Prophet and Iblis, we may conclude that Iblis, as the father of evil on earth, has given clear information in defining the characteristics of the primary enemies of himself and his followers of Jinn and devils. The conflict between Iblis and humankind, which began between him and Prophet Adam, also extends to his hatred of Prophet Muhammad himself. If the Prophet, who never failed to seek refuge and protection of Allah the Almighty, became an object of their hatred and disturbance, then how much worse is the situation for ordinary people?

A common characteristic that enflames hatred and hostility in Iblis and his following of Jinn and devils is goodness and an honorable character, as seen from the fifteen types of enemies to Iblis. Any type of good trait in line with faith and encouraged in Islam will bring out feelings of unease in Iblis and his subordinates, and will undoubtedly become a target of their evil.

It can also be ascertained from the dialogue above that Iblis, the prince of Jinn and devils, possesses the traits of evil, treachery and arrogance. He and his followers are truly like those of the second group mentioned and even consider them as close companions. Whosoever possesses any of those traits and characteristics of the ten companions of Iblis signals that the mission of him and his followers has succeeded to some degree.

Without any shadow of a doubt, humankind has no other choice but to turn to Allah the Almighty, submit themselves to Him, and prepare themselves for an endless battle against Iblis and his minions. Allah the Almighty is the only One for humankind to seek protection and the only place of refuge.

Story of the Prophet meeting Iblis in the mosque

In addition to the abilities and favors given to the Prophet by Allah, he was able to see Iblis and hold dialogues with him. This was another aspect of the *mu'jizat* (prophetic miracles) that

Allah bestowed on him as a Messenger sent as a mercy to all the worlds.

It has been narrated that one day the Prophet of God came to the mosque and saw Iblis beside the mosque's door. The Prophet immediately rebuked him saying, "O Iblis! What are *you* doing here?"

"I wish to enter the mosque in order to disturb someone who is in the middle of prayer, but I am afraid of another person sleeping nearby," replied Iblis.

"O Iblis, why do you not fear the one praying who seeks to bring himself closer to Allah through worship, yet you are afraid of the one asleep who by this very action is neglecting worship?" questioned the Prophet.

"The one praying is ignorant. He does not know the correct manner of prayer, nor does he concentrate when he performs prayer. It is easy for me to ruin his prayer. Whereas the person sleeping is learned. If I ruin the ignorant person's prayer, I fear he will wake the learned one who will then teach him prayer in the correct manner," retorted Iblis.

It can be surmised from this Hadith that it is an inherent characteristic of Iblis and other devils to entice and misguide the Muslim nation from performing worship to Him, Most High.

This is just one of many beneficial stories that have been narrated in order to forewarn humankind and prepare them for the battle against Iblis and his demonic followers.

Humankind is continually exposed to the assaults and evil insinuations of Jinn and devils, even while performing acts of worship to Allah, Most High. Those individuals who do not observe the correct etiquette of *'ibadah* (religious obligations) and adopt a half-hearted attitude towards performing such acts, do not adversely affect the Jinn and devils. In fact, these creatures are more greatly perturbed and fearful of people who possess the capability to spread goodness to others. In short, any act carried out by humankind that brings goodness and honor to the face of the earth causes greater fear in Jinn and devils compared to acts of worship performed by the individual who possesses no firm grounding, direction, or clear intention to gain the pleasure of Allah.

Ibn 'Abbas once said, "Be warned! We (humankind) face four different enemies that you must strive wholeheartedly to defeat. They are:

a. The life of this world. Do not be deceived by worldly pleasures. A verse of the Qur'an states:

    "…let not then this present life deceive you, nor let the Chief Deceiver (Satan) deceive you about Allah."
    (Luqman: 33)

b. Desires of the self. Desire is one of your greatest enemies, as has been mentioned in Allah's book:

    "'Yet I do not absolve myself (of blame): the (human) soul certainly incites evil…'"
    (Yusuf: 53)

c. Jinn devils. These are satanic beings from the Jinn race. Seek Allah's protection from all their evil:

    "Verily Satan is an enemy to you: so treat him as an enemy…"
    (Fatir: 6)

d. Human devils. These are satanic individuals from the human race. Be afraid of this type of devil, for this kind is more evil and more despicable than satanic Jinn. Whereas devils from Jinn seek to misguide humankind by planting doubts in the heart, devils from humankind directly and openly tempt others to evil."

Story of Iblis misguiding humankind by sight

Imam Mujahid said, "The moment a woman appears from the front, Iblis sits on her head to adorn her so that her appearance is pleasing and arousing. Likewise when she appears from behind, Iblis sits on her hips to make them attractive so that they grab the attention of others."

Iblis is continually perched on the eyelids of the children of Adam, ever-waiting for any moment of carelessness. He will never allow the opportunity to slip away of enticing and assailing humankind, and will strive with all his energy to obscure their vision so that they will look at and find pleasing those things that are not good for them. These temptations and suggestions will not cease until they find their outcome in evil and harm to humankind.

"Say to the believing men that they should lower their gaze and guard their modesty: that will make for greater purity for them: and Allah is well-acquainted with all that they do."
(An-Nur: 30)

Believing women are also commanded to guard their vision from those things at which they are not permitted to look, as well as protect their modesty by not indulging in immoral acts.

The Prophet said:

"The glance is an arrow from the arrows of Iblis, which are tipped with poison. Whoever guards his glance out of fear of Allah, then Allah will bless him with *Iman* (faith in Allah) and he will feel the sweetness of Iman in his heart."

Story of the Prophet's birth preventing Iblis ascending the heavens

Before the Prophet was born, devils and Jinn were able to ascend to the heavens as they pleased in order to listen to matters discussed by

Angels. Following the Prophet's auspicious birth where he was sent as a mercy to all the worlds, Iblis and his demonic followers were no longer able to ascend to the firmaments to carry out their heinous missions.

This occurrence was the ultimate proof that since he was a baby—even before in the womb—Prophet Muhammad possessed the signs of being the best of humankind and a leader in this world and the Hereafter. He was bestowed with various *mu'jizat* (prophetic miracles) as a sign of his prophethood throughout his struggle to invite people to Islam.

After the Prophet of Allah's birth, the devils and Jinn attempted to rise up into the sky in order to steal a hearing of the secrets of heaven, but they suddenly fell back to earth. Following this, they returned to their leader Iblis, the prince of darkness (curse of Allah be upon him), and reported the incident that caused pandemonium among them.

After listening to the description of events from his Jinn and demonic minions, Iblis said, "Go out, all of you, to the furthest points east and west of the earth, and investigate the cause that prevented you all from ascending up to the firmaments. What on earth could have possibly happened that gives us such extreme difficulty in stealing the news of heaven?"

Following the command of their prince, the Jinn and devils of Iblis spread out through the earth from east to west, until they arrived at the city of Makkah. It was a terrible shock for them to see that in Makkah the ray of goodness and mercy for all the nations, the Prophet Muhammad had been born and was surrounded by Angels. They could see quite clearly that the light of his goodness radiated upwards towards the heavens.

Following this, the Jinn and devils went back to their leader Iblis and informed him about the reality of the situation. Iblis suddenly shrieked at the top of his voice, "Indeed, the signs show that the mercy to all the worlds and all of mankind has arrived!"

Iblis and his followers are beings created by Allah who have been permitted to live until the Day of Judgment. Although this is the case, on account of the evil they perpetrate on the face of the earth, this long life-span brings no benefit to them whatsoever. As a result, their eternal abode will be in the Hell-Fire.

In fact, their infernal permanent place has been fixed ever since the conflict between Iblis and humankind first began with the enmity of Iblis against Prophet Adam. All this stemmed from the pride and arrogance of Iblis who became the prince of devils and Jinn. It demonstrates clearly that these traits are the source of ruin and destruction for any who follow in the footsteps of Iblis.

It is narrated in the book *Daqa'iqul-Akhbat*, when the moment of Judgment arrives, the Angel of Death ('Izra'il) will come to take Iblis's soul by seizing him until he finally expires. During *sakaratul-maut* (the agony of death), Iblis will let out screams of pain that will be truly terrifying. If there were any human beings left alive on earth at that moment, they would be destroyed solely by the sheer terror of Iblis's cries of agony as the Angel drags out his soul.

Story of Iblis sending out his forces all over the earth

In a narration it is related that Iblis had dispatched his forces comprising of Jinn and devils all over the earth. He then said, "Whoever among you was successful in causing Muslims to stray, I will give him a crown to wear on his head. And whoever caused Muslims to fall and created trouble for them, his position will be raised closer to me, his prince."

Following this, one of his followers stepped forward and stated, "I continually goaded so-and-so until he divorced his wife."

The Prince of Darkness retorted, "This was only a minor evil that has not made me proud, because very soon he will marry again."

Another of Iblis's followers came forward announcing, "I never ceased whispering suggestions to so-and-so until I raised enmity between him and his Muslim brother."

Iblis remonstrated, "You, too, are undeserving of my pleasure, because in the very near future they will be reunited again."

Then a third follower approached Iblis saying, "I persistently enticed so-and-so until he committed illicit sex."

Iblis exclaimed, "Your work is excellent!" Iblis then gave him the crown as a token of gratitude for his evil deeds.

The important lesson that should be noted from this story is that Iblis does not feel satisfied with just any wicked ruses carried out by his followers. Of all the evil and destruction perpetrated by his forces, he continually searches for and evaluates those deeds that wreak maximal damage and loss for humanity.

Story of Iblis declaring himself as 'Isa Al-Masih (Jesus Christ)

It was related by Wahb bin Munabbin of an event that took place before the birth of the noble Prophet Muhammad. There once lived a pious man who never ceased to perform acts of worship day and night. He rarely returned home, due to his whole time being devoted to worshipping Allah in the manner taught by 'Isa Al-Masih (Jesus Christ).

On account of his unceasing good deeds and acts of righteousness, it was inevitable that he could not escape the attention of Iblis who would attempt to make him fall. Nevertheless, it was not a simple task for him to tempt the pious man due to his earnestness and sincerity in following his faith and devotion to religious duties. It was only after a long time of strenuous endeavors to search for the means to misguide him that Iblis finally discovered a way to approach him.

Iblis began his evil mission by continually calling the name of the pious man outside his place of retreat and worship to Allah. The pious man did not entertain Iblis's cries, but just kept quiet and refused to answer. Then Iblis attempted to threaten him, shouting, "If I should leave this place, you will surely regret it!" But Iblis's bluff went unheeded by the ascetic, because he was aware of the deceit and enticement of Iblis.

Iblis saw that his efforts were fruitless. So as a last resort, he claimed that he was Prophet 'Isa.

The man of God replied to him, "If you are 'Isa, did you not command us to always perform acts of worship to Allah wholeheartedly? Did you also not tell us that at a certain moment in time the Day of Judgment will come and it will be the end of this world? So if you have now come with a teaching that is different to these tenets, we will certainly not accept them."

Iblis was now absolutely certain that his efforts would be in vain, so he admitted that he was Iblis whose aim is to seduce and deceive humankind. So the pious man asked him an important question that contains a beneficial wisdom for one and all: "Tell me what is the one characteristic or behavior of the descendants of Prophet Adam that makes it easy for you to cause them to stumble onto the path of misguidance?"

Iblis retorted, "Hard-heartedness! This trait makes it as easy for me and my followers to cause them to stray like a child plays with a ball."

In every character and behavior of humankind, there is always room for Jinn and devils to set a snare that will eventually lead to the ruination and obliteration of a person's future in this world and the Hereafter. The only path to safeguard ourselves from the deceit and evil suggestions of devils is to continually bring ourselves closer to the Lord Most High, so that His blessings and compassion will always be upon us and He will include us among those who receive His protection.

Story of Iblis obstructing the Prophet's night journey

As is generally known, one of the greatest *mu'jizat* (prophetic miracles) of the Prophet Muhammad as a sign of his prophethood was the occasion of his *'Isra* (Night-Journey) and *Mi'raj* (Ascension). He was taken up to *Sidratul-Muntaha* (the Lote-tree in the Seventh Heaven) in order to witness for himself the greatness and majesty of Allah.

This miraculous event is known to the whole of the Muslim Ummah. In the middle of his historic journey accompanied by the Angel Jibril, he was obstructed by an old man, who was Iblis appearing in human form. Iblis was looking for an opportunity to make trouble for the Prophet and disturb his journey to *Sidratul-Muntaha* where he was supposed to attend an audience with Allah, Most Powerful.

The Angel Jibril knew that this person who kept calling over and over again was, in fact, Iblis trying to tempt and deceive Prophet Muhammad. So Jibril said to him, "O Muhammad! Hurry on your journey." "Who is that old man that keeps on calling out?" enquired the Prophet. "He is Allah's enemy, Iblis, may Allah curse him, and he wants you to obey him," said Jibril, adding, "If *you* answer his call, then certainly your Ummah will also submit to and follow him!"

This incident is a clear sign and a poignant lesson for the whole of humanity, and particularly for Muslims as the followers of Muhammad, that Iblis and his minions from Jinn and devils are clearly the greatest enemy they face. Their sole intent on this earth until Doomsday is nothing less than a continuous effort to drag humankind down into the pit of misguidance and unbelief.

Story of Jinn listening to the Prophet recite the Qur'an

The Jinn never knew about the Qur'an until they heard it recited by Prophet Muhammad. After listening to his recitation, which touched their very souls, they became fearful and dazed. Their hearts were truly moved by these verses containing wisdom of great benefit to them as slaves of Allah, Most Powerful.

The verses of the Qur'an captivated them and filled their hearts. As far as our knowledge of them extends, they are like humankind in that they have the ability to choose between right or wrong, faith or unbelief. Therefore, it is not surprising that the miracle of the Qur'an itself, as the Word of Allah, should illuminate and revive their very inner selves to the point that they were no longer able to reject the truth brought by the Prophet Muhammad.

Allah put these invisible beings in a position where they could not escape from the truth. The Arabs of *Jahiliyyah* (the Days of Ignorance) referred to in the Quranic verses about the Jinn used to believe that the Jinn possessed power and greatness all over the earth.

Due to this belief, if they wished to spend the night in a place that was uninhabited, their first and foremost action was to ask protection of the Jinn by honoring or calling them. It was only after doing this that the people of the Days of Ignorance felt secure. They also used to believe that the Jinn had knowledge of the Unseen that they would pass on to shamans who acted as intermediaries between humans and Jinn. Among these shamans were those who worshipped the Jinn and attributed to them a family lineage to Allah.

These and other types of belief in the Jinn were rampant in pagan Arab society of the Days of Ignorance. However, these beliefs have also crept into the realm of our society and continue even up till today.

CHAPTER 3: THE WORLD OF MAGIC AND WITCHCRAFT

The meaning of the words "magic" or "witchcraft" in the simplest terms is any type of evil action aimed at harming others carried out with the aid of unseen beings. Despite the fact that it is evidently evil, Allah has permitted its existence in this world solely as a test and trial for His slaves, although He does not approve of it or its usage.

From one angle, it has been said that magic is solely an incidence of a delusional disturbance or a hallucination. Nevertheless, it *does* occur, and it can have a serious effect on the mind and body of an individual through sickness, as well as the physical and mental symptoms that emerge as a result of it. Even more serious is that it can even lead to death.

Some examples of magic or witchcraft usually practiced nowadays are incantations or spells with the objective of raising mutual hatred between husband and wife, which then results in conflict and divorce.

There are other types of witchcraft carried out by certain individuals who harbor intense feelings of envy towards others. They normally desire to affect the trade or business of others or create a bad image of certain places of trade, which will result in loss or ruin for these businesses.

In addition, there are also magic formulas especially intended to ensure that a young woman will experience difficultly in finding a marriage partner and that no man will propose to her. In the same vein, there are spells that can cause skin disease to break out on a potential bride's face, resulting in her future husband changing his decision to marry her.

A popular type of magic utilized in the world of black arts is that which incorporates the interference of Jinn or devils to give rise to sickness or disability of the body. This may manifest itself in ways such as paralysis of the hands or feet, or even the swelling of the whole body.

Those suffering from these types of sicknesses usually assume that they are forms of conventional illness. However, these illnesses cannot be cured using conventional forms of treatment or medicine. Included among the kinds of witchcraft that affect the physical wellbeing of the person are those whereby a devil or Jinn enters a woman's uterus to block the path of the ovum and prevent her husband's sperm from fertilizing it. This results in her being unable to become pregnant and, in the long run, her being unable to have children at all.

Indications that someone has fallen under the effects of witchcraft include, for example, the sudden instance of someone feeling hatred for his or her spouse without any clear reason, especially in cases where there was no such incident of this happening between the respective spouses previously. Feelings of hatred such as these, which appear all of a sudden and without cause, may be a form of magic that is carried out by an attack from particularly dangerous species of Jinn.

In addition to these, among the various spells and incantations of witchcraft are those that cause an individual to become possessed by a Jinn or devil. Such individuals display behavior such as the desire to be alone followed by violent outbursts and uncontrollable actions. Signs that indicate possession may be seen by changes in the individual's face at different times, which may sometimes be a fiery red color changing to a darker, even more intense color on one side of the face. The afflicted person may experience frightening dreams or nightmares in which they may be heard uttering unintelligible words in their sleep.

Types of deadly magic

Nowadays, the most popular form of witchcraft utilized is that which aims to destroy the fabric of married life between a man and his wife. Among the causes that are the source of hostile relations between spouses, it is said that Jinn possession is one of them. A Jinn may enter the body of one of them, such as the wife—who is normally beautiful in the eyes of her husband—suddenly causing her to look hideous and repulsive. The resulting cold feelings of the husband towards her will continue until they manifest in him a total lack of desire to sleep with her.

The methods of magic that create disturbance between husband and wife take various forms. Certain methods do not involve the interference of Jinn, but they are still, nevertheless, extremely dangerous. This is because these kinds of witchcraft leave a psychological effect on the husband and wife, whereby cold-heartedness is caused by each partner harboring mutual feelings of suspicion during sexual intercourse or one partner experiencing sudden sexual dysfunction.

In addition to all of this, there are also black arts that utilize the disturbance of Jinn and devils to decimate family life. For example, a Jinn will possess one of the spouses in order to bring out negative feelings and bad expectations towards the other spouse. Slowly but surely, they begin to grow apart until they finally separate. This is the most common type of disturbance.

Normally, persons afflicted by witchcraft will, without any apparent reason, become agitated due to a feeling of pain over the whole body. Following this, they will experience a sudden change in their personality, such as an overwhelming desire to be alone, retreating into fantasies or delusions, and displaying totally unexpected behavior.

In addition, they will experience frequent terrifying dreams and unstable sleep patterns marked by restlessness, as well as confused and disordered talking in their sleep or delirium that is unintelligible. Disturbances of this sort may continue until they eventually manifest into a serious psychological problem for those affected. Despite this, we can determine whether the problem is related to witchcraft or elements of Jinn possession by analyzing the afflicted person through several methods.

Magic can be divided into several distinct categories. First, one type of witchcraft is practiced utilizing elements from nature, such as special properties from specific ingredients known by the practitioner of magic but unknown to the victim of magic. Second, another type is illusion or "sleight of hand" in which the secret lies in the quickness of the hand by hiding one thing and showing something else. A third type is magic that controls the mind by influencing weak-minded people through methods such as hypnotism. However, the effect of these forms of magic is not as damaging to humankind compared to inference of Jinn and devils.

There is still, however, a question that needs to be answered: how are Jinn or devils able to enter the human body? If it is surprising enough that they are able to enter and possess a person, even more disturbing is how are they able to settle and multiply in specific parts throughout the areas of the body?

In fact, this question was answered by the Prophet 1,400 years ago. In a Hadith narrated by Sayyidah Safiyyah bint Huyay, the Prophet of Allah said:

"Satan moves through the body of the children of Adam in the same way as blood flows through it."

As previously mentioned, Jinn and devils have been created possessing various special powers and abilities that are not always easy to be understood by the human mind.

Examples are their varying sizes, ability to transform their shapes, life-span, method of movement, etc. Therefore, it should come as no surprise that they do not face problems when they attack humankind using diverse methods that humans are unable to resist. They are able to slip into the human body in the same way electric current flows through cable wires.

Those who have already made their way throughout the human body, in the same way blood flows through it, will usually cause disturbance and difficulties to the life of the individual. They will control the mind and heart of the person until the condition results in tension and stress, loss of memory and thought processes, loss of all desires and the will to live, unconsciousness, and even in certain cases death.

Factors why Jinn enter into the human body

Many differing factors encourage Jinn to enter inside the human body resulting in various conditions and disturbances that cause suffering to people. One of the most prominent contributing factors is the character of the person in question, such as the individual who is neglectful of righteous deeds and does not keep a close connection to Allah.

People who do not ever apply themselves in doing good set themselves up as the most exposed target to the harassment and evil designs of Jinn and devils. Another reason is the actions or steps taken by an individual that produce a negative effect on them, whether carried out intentionally or otherwise. For example, when someone accidentally destroys their dwellings or pours boiling water over places where they may be—without mentioning Allah's name—causing the death of the Jinn's or devils' children.

Overcoming interference by Jinn

Magic or witchcraft, according to the general understanding, involves actions performed by a person according to specific stipulations under conditions and prerequisites that are shrouded in mystery.

It should be noted that the practice of magic is solely for the purpose of perpetrating evil and immorality, and it has different levels.

In general, the ultimate effect of this type of magic is to cause short-term physical and mental problems or long-term ones resulting in death. It is not improbable that it may even cause someone to die suddenly and unexpectedly.

Ordinarily, those affected by witchcraft or the black arts display an apparent change externally and internally, such as instability of mind or mental problems. In brief, the symptoms that may be observed from victims of magic include a mental state that is highly disturbed and out of control.

By way of example, consider the art of casting love charms to mesmerize a woman. The victim will experience symptoms such as irrational behavior whereby, in certain situations, she could be observed talking to herself and laughing out loud as if she were ecstatically happy. Sometimes and without any apparent reason, she will sit in front of a mirror continuously for hours in the middle of the night beautifying herself, even wearing new clothes, as if she is a bride waiting to go to her wedding. Moreover, at any time she may unexpectedly display violent outbursts in which she will scream continuously and tear up her clothes.

The result of such witchcraft on a victim is a massive mental disintegration, resulting in a total loss of sanity and rational thinking.

These forms of witchcraft may be classified under the group of magic and black arts that practice the making of offerings and the worship of figures made from candles or from the personal effects and articles taken from the intended victim.

In reality, the strength and ability to defeat these harmful effects is a hidden secret and wisdom. It is not a power and advantage that can be grasped by every person. Surrender and reliance on God, on its own, is not enough as the sole, absolute path to overcome problems brought on by magic and witchcraft. The true strength lies in du'a (supplications to Allah), which are read at the time treatment takes place, and are personally and directly connected with the religious observances of the individual who is carrying out treatment of the problems.

As witchcraft or any of the black arts can directly affect the soul and inner being of the human, it follows that the only beneficial path to face this risk is to prepare and further empower one's inner strength.

Symptoms of Jinn and devil possession, or what is normally called "hysteria" in most societies of the world, cause the victim to manifest abnormal behavior such as screaming, delirium, fleeing from others, and similar actions.

If this situation occurs among a group involving many people, it is referred to as hysteria. Conversely, if the same type of attack affects only an individual, it is termed "spirit possession."

The individual victim of an attack of hysteria will usually have a background of extended emotional stress and pent-up negative feelings. Despite this, there is also a large number who do not have a prior history of emotional disturbance or extended stress, yet they too fall victim to attacks of hysteria.

Usually, those who are suspected of being possessed by a supernatural being do not possess any elements of emotionally disturbed feelings in their personality. On the contrary, there are suppositions that claim the disturbances they undergo are a result of certain actions they did, regardless as to whether they were aware or unaware of such at the time.

An example of such action would be when a person unintentionally destroys the residence of a Jinn, as well as various other actions that hurt the Jinn. These types of incidents will raise their anger and impel them to attack, possess, and harm the individual in question. Aside of this kind of situation, the individual who may be possessed and controlled by this type of unseen creature may also be susceptible to the harm of witchcraft instigated by others who are motivated by feelings of hatred or envy.

Hysteria and Jinn possession both display similar recognizable elements. Psychological factors, such as emotional problems and mental stress, basically form external symptoms that make the person more susceptible to attacks of hysteria or devil possession.

The same applies to different problems such as tension in the workplace, family difficulties, and similar troubles. Any form of stress that involves mental disruption, which leads to an unstable mind and emotional state, is the indicator that the person is in a highly exposed position to possible interference or attack by supernatural beings.

Victims of magic may sometimes experience temporary insanity or mental problems, as well as behavior resembling victims of hysteria or Jinn and demonic possession. This is a form of attack that involves disturbance of the mental thought processes.

There are, in addition, other types of magic that involve physical attacks. These are easier to recognize compared to hysteria or devil possession. Witchcraft that is aimed at the mental state is extremely difficult to detect, except by observing symptoms of change in the victim, which differ considerably in comparison to conventional symptoms indicative of an individual's state of health.

Witchcraft that involves the physical state particularly affects specific parts of the body. For example, when the stomach suddenly swells up, or the feet swell up causing the inability to walk, or the eyes become blurred to the extent that vision is undermined, and various other kinds of disturbances.

Symptoms of interference by Jinn

Among the indications that a person is being subjected to mental disturbance as a result of being attacked by unseen creatures is difficulty in sleeping or frequent attacks of insomnia during the night whereby the mind becomes confused and highly disturbed. These individuals have a constant feeling as if there is a creature they cannot see pressing down on top of them while they sleep, to the point they are unable to move. In this panic-ridden state, they are unable call for help or attempt to defend themselves. In more critical situations, the individual has great difficulty in breathing. These people often laugh, cry, or scream while sleeping. In some cases, they may even sleepwalk.

All the while, their mind and thoughts become increasingly strained. Each moment they are assailed by dreams in which they see glimpses of human figures with strange faces—dark, and with fangs and horns. These images they are forced to see in such dreams appear the moment they close their eyes to sleep. They suffer these same dreams over and over again, until they reach the stage where they cannot sleep and feel extreme tension.

In addition to seeing strange beings, they also have dreams in which they see frightening, vicious animals like dogs, snakes, tigers, etc. Although there are some people in this condition who are quite normal, even they complain of being unable to sleep. On their bodies, particularly the areas of the shins, thighs, or arms, they may feel weak as a result of patches of blue bruises, which are very painful.

Supernatural beings, whether Iblis himself or other devils, always appear in frightening forms. By the permission of Allah, they can also transform themselves into various different shapes of animals such as snakes or bears, or savage or poisonous animals that cause anxiety and terror. It is only at these moments humankind can see the presence of Jinn.

Other than these manifestations, humankind is unable to see Jinn in their true, original form.

In these manifestations, they usually appear in a completely black form, because the color black signifies strength and the terrifying force of evil.

As these manifestations take on the shapes of animals that cause fear when seen, it is clear that the intention is to disturb and to frighten humankind.

In addition to the other symptoms experienced by victims of witchcraft, it is known that while they are in a deep state of sleep they dream of entering a different, unknown world. Here they see various types of strange and frightening beings.

In reality, the scenes they are witnessing are in the realm of the Jinn; they have been transported to the Jinn's world. Among some of these victims, their spirits are forced to carry out heavy tasks while in the dream-state of this Jinn world. Although they experience this dimension in the dream, when they awake from sleep they actually feel the physical effects resulting from this to the point of extreme tiredness or exhaustion.

Other victims among them have undergone disturbances by continually seeing strange figures or shadows around their places of residence. Sometimes these figures resemble someone well-known to them.

They may also experience interference in the form of unusual sounds, such as the movement of someone walking on the roof of their house. They may suddenly hear the sound of a tap or a light-switch being turned on, but in fact there is no one else present in the house at that moment.

These kinds of disturbances under normal circumstances may usually be dismissed as just occasional occurrences. However, on account of their constant repetition, they cause the victim to remain in a state of anxiety and worry. They may even see venomous creatures in the house, such as poisonous centipedes, scorpions, etc., or hear the distant sound of a dog howling eerily in the middle of the night.

Occasionally, they may come across creatures in their houses not usually encountered, such as caterpillars, grasshoppers, worms, flies, etc., in large numbers.

In other situations, they can smell aromas or odors of which the source is unknown, such as extremely sweet, fragrant aromas, or even foul odors like pus, blood, or the stench of drains. They may also sense that they see in a lightning-fast glance another being who is continually observing their movements.

They may feel sickness or weakness over the whole body or in specific parts, but when they are examined by a doctor, they are confirmed as being normal and not suffering from any form of illness.

In addition, they may experience feelings of uneasiness, headaches, swelling, heat around the ears, and the sensation of the hair on the back of the neck standing on end. They may sometimes experience disturbances of hearing where they suddenly hear sounds like the wind, waves, bells, people talking, or just noise. On other occasions, those afflicted may hear music that does not cease. These situations may occur when those affected are in a specific part of the house in which they live.

In more serious cases, they may even feel unable to perform religious devotions such as mentioning the name of Allah, which prevents them from performing *salat* (five Muslim daily prayers), reading the Qur'an, and other acts of worship. They may become incapable of remembering the recitations that used to be routine for them, or feel sad, depressed, and tearful each time they desire to pray or recite the Qur'an. They may even feel sick or drowsy when they attempt these obligations.

In their day-to-day lives, they feel continuous, heavy stress that becomes more acute when they are up against problems. These feelings even occur when they are facing issues, or the moment they brood on issues that are not major problems. They may all of a sudden feel "empty" and unable to think of anything.

People who are struck with disturbances like these normally suffer certain physical symptoms that they are unable to comprehend, such as the sensation of the throat being strangled and the inability to swallow food or drink. Their fingertips may feel numb, and there may be a sensation as if something is continually moving about within their blood vessels. They may feel as if their chest is being struck with a heavy object while their head feels as if it is being clutched in the vice-grip of a solid object.

In reality, there are many different examples of individuals who have become victims of interference or attack by Jinn through witchcraft. In addition to those already mentioned, there is also the instance of the victim who is unconscious and lies rigid like a dead person. Certain parts of the body display symptoms like that of a corpse, such as extreme coldness in the feet and particularly at the ends of the toes. The eyes are tightly closed, displaying only slight movement beneath the eyelids. There may be an object located between the two eyebrows that resembles an extra eye, which continually moves about observing the surrounding area.

In addition to these types of victims, we may also find those who are in a normal condition but are prone to extreme aggression and screaming. If people come too close to them, they will become agitated, demanding to be left alone. Those closest to them may be at risk of harm from them.

In more critical cases, we find those who appear to be normal but, in fact, are in a state of mind that is highly disturbed, disappointed with life, and preoccupied with suicide.

In certain cases, those afflicted will complain of pain in the area of the heart, such as patients suffering from heart conditions, or pain around the skull, such as those with brain tumors.

Yet in cases of suffering from the effects of magic such as this, the victims are not really experiencing problems with the heart or brain like actual patients in hospital who have been diagnosed with these conditions. However, the interference of Jinn and devils who assail with pain resembling heart attacks or brain tumors normally causes the victim to undergo the same magnitude of suffering undergone by actual patients who have been confirmed with these conditions by medical technology.

From another angle, situations such as these are not an indication that all patients with heart conditions or brain tumors became ill due to the interference of Jinn. What is clear, however, is that attacks and disturbances of Jinn and devils can result in the victim displaying identical symptoms experienced by typical patients of these illnesses.

The most fundamental principle in handling victims of Jinn attacks, who suffer illness as a result of interference that stems from witchcraft, is through treatment that separates or exorcises unseen beings while at the same time stops them from causing further harm to humankind.

In addition to this principle, it should be emphasized that whoever aims to treat the person who has become a victim of interference and attacks such as these must possess a personal background that is sound and strong. Inner strength such as this does not just involve the physical aspect, but much more importantly, it requires spiritual strength. This is because the person carrying out treatment of the victim is not dealing with an individual from the physical aspect *per se*, but rather with the supernatural creature that has possessed him or her and is invisible to the naked eye. On account of this invisibility, which hinders the one treating the victim from knowing and recognizing this enemy, it becomes difficult to estimate and measure the strength and actual character of the being to be exorcised from the victim's body.

During the treatment process, the one carrying it out will usually notice that the victim's pulse rate will be higher than normal. This is one of the reactions or indications that the sick person is being subjected to disturbance from Jinn inside the body. In situations such as these, it is important that the one carrying out the treatment keeps in mind to take each step very carefully in order to prevent the patient from reacting violently, creating an uncontrollable situation. The patient's reactions may differ vastly, taking the form of struggling and fierce screaming, cursing and swearing, defiance and spitting, or kicking and other similar actions.

Some patients will squirm as if they are in pain and make snorting noises, and then let out an extremely unusual gruff voice. Sometimes the voice will sound like an old person, even though the actual patient may be young.

The creature inside the patient's body may sometimes even refuse to communicate or give any form of response. There may be several possible reasons for this. One reason may be that the illness is not caused by interference by supernatural beings. It may have occurred as a result of a previous injury, virus infection, etc., causing damage to specific organs or nerves.

The sickness may also be based on an extreme case of interference, in which the being has permanently entrenched itself, becoming one with the patient's body.

Based on these reasons, we must constantly be wary and on our guard against the evil of magic and the forces of darkness. Certain measures that are highly encouraged must be adopted as a shield to protect oneself.

A permanent and continuous practice of religious obligations must be adopted, particularly performing the five daily prayers and the following actions:

- Make it a familiar habit to recite *"A'udhu billahi minash-shaitanir-rajim"* (I seek refuge in Allah from Satan, the accursed) for Allah's protection.
- Read passages from the Qur'an at least once a day.
- Avoid any form of magic completely.
- Do not involve oneself in the affairs of the Unseen, particularly Jinn.
- Believe wholeheartedly in Allah as it is only He Who has absolute power to protect us from the threats and disturbances of devils, Jinn, and humans.

It may be recalled that the original creation of Jinn and devils was from flaming fire. Therefore, in order to overcome the strength of these unseen beings, any force whose element is fire must be wiped out or prevented from causing further destruction.

Among the beneficial information required to defeat the interference of a Jinn who enters the human body, observation of the traits and character of the Jinn is of paramount importance. Jinn that carry out possession are probably the most stubborn and cruel-hearted of their species. These characteristics may be ascertained from their desire to remain in the human body.

With regard to beating aimed at driving the Jinn or devil out of the body, this may be carried out particularly on the shoulders and back, hands and feet, or fingers and toes. As has already been pointed out, the effects of beating will not be felt at all by the human individual, but only by the Jinn inside his or her body. As a precautionary step, each strike should be accompanied by recitation from the Qur'an.

It is also necessary to constantly observe the individual, because each reaction from him or her during the beating process will mirror the effect on the Jinn inside. If there are more than one Jinn inside the body, they will constantly shift about inside the patient in order to lighten the blows against them and also in an effort to deceive the one treating the victim. There are also Jinn that are experienced in possessing a human and that will attempt to flee when the victim is being treated. However, the moment the person treating the patient has departed, the Jinn will re-enter the patient's body.

There are also among the Jinn those who have tremendous strength and perseverance in remaining inside the human body. Sometimes these Jinn may even attempt to negotiate their situation by demanding food or other things from the one treating the victim.

In fact, when a situation like this takes place, it becomes extremely hard to exorcise the Jinn. One method by which we may recognize the character and strength of this type of Jinn is through recitation of verses from the Qur'an. The moment we begin to read the Holy Qur'an, the victim's eyes will become full of tears, and he or she will then cry and sob without any clear reason. This is a clear indication of a body possessed by a Jinn whose size may be small, but it is still very strong, evil, and stubborn.

There is another method in which the force of the Jinn is allowed to live, but it cannot function in such a way that causes harm and destruction to people. This situation may be likened to the flame of darkness that is allowed to burn, but is weak when up against the pure light of goodness.

The way to gain the upper hand over the flame of evil is by readying and strengthening the light inside oneself. The only method to attain this is by bringing oneself closer to Allah and to be consistent in acts of worship that will increase one's personal strength—inner or outer.

In the long run, all this must be supported by continuous reliance on Allah and du'a to Him, so that He will protect and safeguard us from any threat from Jinn or devils during the treatment of victims of disturbance or attack through witchcraft. It is clear that resistance against magic is a battle between two forces: the flame of evil and the pure light of goodness.

Treating victims of magic

Both the victim of witchcraft and the person carrying out the treatment must have firm-heartedness and a resolute spirit, combined with complete total surrender in and sincere du'a to Allah. Acts of worship for this purpose are not solely to seek a cure, but also to gain the support of Allah at all times. Religious acts performed by the patient to seek Allah's favor with the sole aim of being cured put the situation at risk, due to an insincere intention based on total self-interest.

Qualities of the one giving treatment

In addition to firm-heartedness and bringing oneself closer to Allah, the person who intends to carry out the treatment must also embody firm spiritual stability. This is through avoidance and protecting oneself from falling into sins, particularly major sins. In addition to this, a sincere character that truly seeks Allah's pleasure is absolutely essential, for it may be comparable to a firm fortress that stands against the evil of Jinn that is extremely complex to outmaneuver.

To take on the responsibility of treating the victim of witchcraft, it is an imperative prerequisite to have the correct knowledge and practice that conforms and is in harmony with the Shari'ah (Laws of Islam), without exceeding its defined limits.

This important point must be taken into consideration, because among persons treating victims of magic are those who resort to seeking the aid of other Jinn in order to chase out the actual Jinn affecting the victim they are treating at that time. For example, they use the help of Jinn or they utter incantations or formulas that idolize the Jinn or something else besides Allah. If this kind of scenario occurs, it is not unusual that the patient's condition will deteriorate and even reach a critical level. It is also quite possible that, in addition to the victim, this negative effect will rebound against the person carrying out the treatment.

Therefore, the character and background of the one performing the treatment play a significant role in determining the possibility of recovery for the victim. It is imperative that he be of a character that continually carries out acts of righteousness, has knowledge and experience, possesses a sincere intention and—last but not least—a serious personal commitment and desire to aid the victim of the black arts. These traits will consolidate the personal strength and determination of the individual to overcome any difficult experience encountered while up against the evil force of Jinn that possess the human body.

When the two spiritual elements of Jinn and the person of pious character meet, it is certain that an intense clash will result. However, by the permission of Allah and through His protection and strength, the moment the force of the evil Jinn is aware of the power of the one performing treatment, the Jinn will not be able to stand up against it. Nevertheless, during the first stages of treatment the evil forces of Jinn will refuse to surrender and admit defeat. They will resort to deception by putting forward numerous reasons and excuses aimed at creating confusion. They will also behave in many different ways. All this is designed to frustrate the efforts of the person carrying out treatment and make him feel unsuccessful. However, through patience and sincerity, by the permission of Allah he will succeed in exorcising the power of evil from the body of the victim it is controlling.

Close connection between Jinn and witchcraft

"They followed what the satans recited over Solomon's kingdom. Solomon did not disbelieve, but the satans disbelieved, teaching men magic, and such things as came down at Babylon to the angels Harut and Marut. But neither of these taught

anyone (such things) without saying: 'We are only for trial; so do not blaspheme.' They learned from them the means to sow discord between man and wife. But they could not thus harm anyone except by Allah's permission. And they learned what harmed them, not what profited them. And they knew that the buyers (of magic) would have no share in the happiness of the Hereafter. And vile was the price for which they did sell their souls, if they but knew!"

(Al-Baqarah: 102)

Stories about magic and the black arts are likely to shock and stun many people, due to the ruination and evil that results from the practice of magic.

Many people believe, albeit at a subconscious level, that Jinn and devils know many secrets of the Unseen that are unknown to humankind. It is the effect of this belief that results in humankind being gradually pulled under the influence and deception of devils, until they are caught within this deviation and finally they take Satan as their advisor and guide to their path in this world.

The Qur'an has successively recorded a number of stories involving the stand of Allah's Messengers against magic throughout the ages. For instance, Prophet Sulaiman was accused of being an unbeliever because he could communicate with devils. However, Allah had always protected him from unbelief. In reality it was the devils who were unbelievers, and it was they who taught magic to humankind with the aim of creating division between husband and wife. Satan knew that the family is the foundation of a sound society. The breakdown of the family institution in any society would result in the ultimate destruction of the whole society.

In another verse of the Qur'an, Allah informs us about the actions of devils who attempt to steal information from the heavens, resulting in them being chased away by shooting stars:

"And We have (from of old) adorned the lowest heaven with Lamps, and We have made such (Lamps as) missiles to drive away satans, and have prepared for them the Punishment of the Blazing Fire."
(Al-Mulk: 5)

Among the annals of history witnessed in the Qur'an regarding stories connected to magic, we find the record of events that took place between Musa (Moses) and the sorcerers of Pharaoh:

> "And We showed Pharaoh all Our Signs, but he did reject and refuse. He said: 'Hast thou come to drive us out of our land with thy magic, O Moses? But we can surely produce magic to match thine! So make a tryst between us and thee, which we shall not fail to keep—neither we nor thou—in a place where both shall have even chances.' Moses said: 'Your tryst is the Day of the Festival, and let the people be assembled when the sun is well up.' So Pharaoh withdrew: he concerted his plan, and then came (back). Moses said to them: 'Woe to you! Forge not ye a lie against Allah, lest He destroy you (at once) utterly by chastisement: the forger must suffer failure!' So they disputed, one with another, over their affair, but they kept their talk secret. They said: 'These two are certainly (expert) magicians: their object is to drive you out from your land with their magic, and to do away with your most cherished ways. Therefore concert your plan, and then assemble in (serried) ranks: he wins (all along) today who gains the upper hand.' They said: 'O Moses! Whether wilt

thou that thou throw (first) or that we be the first to throw?' He said: 'Nay, throw ye first!' Then behold their ropes and their rods—so it seemed to him on account of their magic—began to be in lively motion! So Moses conceived in his mind a (sort of) fear. We said: 'Fear not! For thou hast indeed the upper hand: throw that which is in thy right hand: quickly will it swallow up that which they have faked: what they have faked is but a magician's trick: and the magician succeeds not.' So the magicians were thrown down to prostration: they said, 'We believe in the Lord of Aaron and Moses.' (Pharaoh) said: "Believe ye in Him before I give you permission? Surely this must be your leader, who has taught you magic! Be sure I will cut off your hands and feet on opposite sides, and I will have you crucified on trunks of palm-trees: so shall ye know for certain, which of us can give the more severe and the more lasting punishment!' They said: 'Never shall we prefer thee to what has come to us of Clear Signs, or than Him Who created us! So decree whatever thou desirest to decree: for thou canst only decree (touching) the life of this world. For us, we have believed in our Lord: may He forgive us our faults,

and the magic to which thou didst compel us: for Allah is Best and Most Abiding.' Verily he who comes to his Lord as a sinner (at Judgment),—for him is Hell: therein shall he neither die nor live. But such as come to Him as Believers who have worked righteous deeds,—for them are ranks exalted,—Gardens of Eternity, beneath which flow rivers: they will dwell therein for aye: such is the reward of those who purify themselves (from evil)."
(Taha: 56–76)

It was not the magic of Jinn that Allah caused to come through Prophet Musa when he stood against Pharaoh and his sorcerers. It was a *mu'jizat* (prophetic miracle) of Allah to teach the sorcerers that the only power able to remove and obliterate their black arts is the power of Allah Most High, the Lord of all humankind.

Indeed the only refuge and only One to be relied on from the evil of devils is Allah, Lord of power. No one other than Him has the power to protect His slaves from the wickedness and disturbances of Jinn and devils.

"In the case of those who say, 'Our Lord is Allah', and, further, stand straight and

steadfast, the angels descend on them (from time to time): 'Fear ye not!' (they suggest), 'Nor grieve! But receive the Glad Tidings of the Garden (of Bliss), the which ye were promised! We are your protectors in this life and in the Hereafter: therein shall ye have all that ye shall desire; therein shall ye have all that ye ask for!—A hospitable gift from One Oft-Forgiving, Most Merciful!' Who is better in speech than one who calls (men) to Allah, works righteousness, and says, 'I am of those who bow in Islam'? Nor can Goodness and Evil be equal. Repel (Evil) with what is better: then will he between whom and thee was hatred become as it were thy friend and intimate! And no one will be granted such goodness except those who exercise patience and self-restraint,—none but persons of the greatest good fortune. And if (at any time) an incitement to discord is made to thee by Satan, seek refuge in Allah. He is the One Who hears and knows all things."
(Fussilat:30–36)

The pull of the world of witchcraft

It is a widespread trait of people to be attracted by things that are unusual and amazing. Certain people choose to learn the black arts or witchcraft because of the fantastic power they may possess thereby. It is ironic that despite the fact that devils are the most loathsome of creations, there are still very many people who wish to become their companions in order to gain a power that is not possessed by ordinary people. Although some of these people understand and are fully aware that this knowledge goes against all that is right, the power and thrill that comes with it blinds them against making the correct choice between right and wrong.

Islam teaches its followers that they should never take the enemies of Allah, i.e., devils and Jinn who spread mischief over the face of the earth, as companions or, worse still, put them in positions whereby they seek help from them. Although at first glance, it seems that humankind may be able to gain benefit from contact with unseen creatures such as Jinn and demons, in reality the capabilities and amazing gifts of these beings cannot be controlled by human power, because it is their nature to deceive humankind. Those who follow the black arts and magic may derive some benefit from these Jinn, but they themselves cannot escape from becoming a victim of their interference and attacks.

Among those who practice and study witchcraft are people whose aim is to harm others by ordering the Jinn to attack them, thereby causing incurable sickness, insanity, or death.

Others practice magic to treat illnesses. There are also individuals who do not practice magic, but on account of them becoming sick due to Jinn possession and subsequently recovering after several weeks or so, they gain the ability to treat the illnesses of others with the aid of Jinn.

There are also Jinn who bring goodness to humankind without them being aware of it.

Whatever the case, no matter how powerful those who practice the black arts may be, they are unable to go beyond the boundaries limited by normal human failings. If, for instance, they are involved in evil in the shape of crime and subsequently they are arrested and sentenced to prison, the power of their magic and the Jinn or devils from which they sought help will be unable to assist them in overcoming or escaping the existing laws in the world.

In addition to this, there may also be a small group of individuals who have never shown any interest in or ever learned magic consciously or otherwise, yet they sense that there is some kind of extraordinary power inside them that they gained without any conscious effort on their part. They may even be completely aware that there is an unusual kind of power inside them.

Companionship with the Jinn brings great risk to humankind, because once the pledge of friendship is sealed it is exceedingly difficult to break.

Unfortunately, this companionship does not end with the death of the human involved, because the Jinn will then seek a new "heir" among the friends or family of the deceased. It should, therefore, come as no surprise if we hear hair-raising stories of certain individuals known as being companions of Jinn or, as they are usually referred to, those who keep Jinn.

What is more disturbing is that there have been eye-witnesses in such cases who claim that they have seen these deceased individuals return to their homes. However, the being they have seen returning home is, in fact, the deceased person's Jinn companion materializing in his or her form. Since it is extremely difficult to differentiate between these two separate beings, this has led society to assume that a situation such as this is an example of a "haunting" by a "ghost of the dead."

There have also been reports of eerie and macabre situations taking place whereby the dead bodies of individuals who had learned the black arts in life suddenly rose up and even partook of food and drink. Yet it is seldom known by ordinary people that these practitioners of the unseen arts in life used to keep Jinn, and it is these same Jinn who enter and control their bodies in such situations.

In taking advantage of the gifts and powers that they have been given, Jinn and devils are able to materialize in forms identical to people newly deceased. Usually, they will pass in a glance among crowds of people or appear in places that are dim or gloomy. It is in this manner that Jinn and devils will trick people into believing what they are actually seeing truly exists. In truth, there is no such word in Islamic terminology for "ghost of the dead."

The example of the person who practices the black arts or magic by keeping Jinn in order to use their assistance can be compared to the person who takes care of people who are unstable and mentally ill. Even though at certain times they may be able to ask the aid of the Jinn they keep, nevertheless at *any* time they may be attacked by those self-same Jinn.

There are a number of extraordinary feats or abilities within the capability of those people who learn the black arts of keeping Jinn, which they use with the aim of demonstrating their power to others. One example is the ability to bury themselves underground and then emerge after several days with no ill effects.

They also have the ability to fly in the air at the same height as trees. Others may have boiling oil poured over their bodies without any resulting injury. There is no doubt that such amazing power will bring adulation and applause from the audience witnessing such entertainment.

Yet despite all this, the very basis of their power is obtained from the Jinn. Therefore, it is not unusual that these very Jinn, whose mission is to fool and misguide all of humankind, will still strive to pull even them—the dedicated seekers of the black arts—into the trap of evil and humiliation. These people will become arrogant and conceited because of the power and abilities they possess. Some of them may

even join certain groups—or may even be paid—
to commit crimes against others. Yet despite all
this, how bitter a pill it will be for them to swallow
the moment they are caught for their crimes
and receive justice; when they suddenly find the
power and abilities they gained from the aid of
the Jinn no longer function and consequently
cannot alleviate their situation in the slightest.

It cannot be denied that Allah created Jinn
and devils with amazing advantages that truly
dazzle the eyes of humans. These special powers
with which they are equipped make human
beings desirous of possessing them.

Nevertheless, all these advantages and
powers have only come about by the permission
of Allah. Without His permission, no one may
carry out any form of action, even to the level of
breathing. In the same way, Allah will continue
to allow the Jinn and devils to use these abilities
in their quest to destroy humankind in the
manner that their prince, Iblis, promised to
misguide all of humankind, but only until the
Day of Judgment.

Based on this principle, if Jinn had been
created on this earth with a tangible form in the
same manner as human beings, undoubtedly

there would have been large-scale destruction or genocide of humankind. This would have been due to a scenario where human beings were surrounded by Jinn and devils unceasingly committing acts of evil, eventually leading to humankind becoming the victims of their wicked and immoral actions. Humankind would not have been able to survive very long under terrifying and agonizing uncertain circumstances such as these. However, through the mercy and wisdom of Allah, humankind and Jinn may both survive in this world.

Examples of honoring or worshipping Jinn are not solely found among human societies of this day and age. History also records the practice existing among humankind throughout the ages.

Before the light of Islam, the majority among Arab society in *Jahiliyyah* (the Days of Ignorance) venerated and worshipped Jinn. On account of the superstition and pagan beliefs prevalent among them, many idols were built especially for worship and religious rites. Idol-worship formed the largest part of their religious rituals.

Today, we often hear of people in various different places whose background is Muslim, but they have become influenced by the trickery of Jinn and devils to the point that they honor and worship idols in order to secure good luck or help from them.

In fact, these idols or any objects of worship when honored and idolized by humankind will, at some point, begin to display their "power and abilities."

The explanation of this is that while these idols or other relics are intrinsically ordinary objects, there will come a time when religious rituals and worship associated with them will invite the presence of Jinn and devils. In several different Asian societies, such as within the Malay Archipelago, there is a belief in the existence of the *penunggu*, a spirit or force that guards a specific place, object, or idol of worship. In reality, devils and Jinn are very desirous of honor and worship.

Many stories are heard that involve the power and eerie happenings associated with idols, places, or objects that human beings have set up to be venerated and worshipped.

Nevertheless, there are still many people who do not believe in happenings connected to the

Unseen through Jinn and devils. These same people may acknowledge their existence, but they do not take seriously the ability of Jinn to cause harm to humankind.

There are also others who derive pleasure in cursing unseen beings, probably with the intention of challenging them or for other reasons. However, actions such as cursing or reviling them with evil words only acts as a kind of fuel that serves to give them more power. It is not improbable that their size and strength will increase at the time they are cursed and reviled by human beings.

With regard to idols that have become objects of veneration and worship by others, one should beware not to insult or do anything offensive to them in case there may be an unseen being resident inside them. One should never go so far as to underestimate them; even laughing at them could put one at risk of disturbance by Jinn.

The method to overcome them is by asking help from Allah and by demonstrating a polite manner. It is important to avoid negative behavior such as cursing, challenging, and reviling them, for this could result in them becoming increasingly more powerful and fiercer.

In several countries in Asia, particularly Indonesia, there are practitioners of the black arts who have mastered the skill of capturing Jinn in bottles. This ability has been demonstrated on the Indonesian television channel, LATiVi. Indonesia is well-known as one of the most powerful countries in the practice of magic, as well as in the treatment of mysterious illnesses, in addition to certain other countries such as Thailand, India, and America.

If, for instance, in our own houses we should discover signs indicating the presence of strange beings, we must avoid harsh talk and challenging them, because under unfavorable circumstances they may attack us forthwith.

When Jinn appear in human form, the moment we meet them we may not be aware that they are Jinn. However, when it dawns on us that they are actually Jinn, they will hide themselves from us. This means that the second they realize that we have become conscious of their true identity, they will immediately vanish from sight.

Nowadays in many different places, we may witness people displaying skills and extraordinary actions that logically defy normal human capabilities. Yet these actions will no longer seem amazing to us when we become aware that whoever has a bond of companionship with or asks help from the Jinn, these self-same Jinn have the capability to help those people perform feats that go even beyond what we or others have witnessed. In reality, there are no such human beings who possess unusual powers that go beyond the scope of sane reasoning, except in cases where Allah has aided His Messengers. Therefore, any extraordinary acts carried out by practitioners of witchcraft are nothing other than feats performed through the help of the Jinn.

In this age, the majority of people who witness these kinds of actions and display are totally dazzled by them and perceive them to be true. Yet it could never be denied that all these acts and demonstrations only take place through the aid and interference of Jinn.

The average person never usually stops to consider the consequences that result from the practice of black arts or magic. Almost all of the individuals themselves involved in the world of black arts never ponder or are unaware of the terrible fate that will eventually befall them. Whether it comes upon them sooner or later is not the question at hand. However, it is sure that they will never be able to escape from the disturbance and attacks of these Jinn and devils, because it is their very nature to cause harm and evil on earth.

People who practice these arts are at a very high risk of horrifying disturbances and attacks by Jinn, such as paralysis of the whole body like a person at the point of death; others may experience unconsciousness or insanity. If they were truly aware of the disaster that was going to befall them, it would have been a shocking deterrent for many of them to avoid the black arts.

Although in this world Jinn have mastery over abilities and powers far beyond those of human beings, in the Hereafter the situation will be reversed. From certain aspects there may be similarities between humankind and Jinn, but there are also many traits and characteristics created in Jinn that are totally in contradiction with those of human beings.

Soothsayers and fortune tellers

The Prophet Muhammad has clearly forbidden his nation of followers to put their trust in shamans and soothsayers, because the knowledge and news of the Unseen that they pass on to people comes from the evil suggestions of Jinn and devils.

In a Hadith of Bukhari, 'Abdullah Ibn Mas'ud stated, "Allah's Prophet forbade people the price of dogs, the dowry resulting from illicit sex, and the pleasing words of soothsayers and fortune tellers."

In another narration, when the Prophet was asked about shamans and fortune tellers, he replied, "There is no benefit in them." Someone from his Companions then asked him further, "O Prophet of God! Is it not so that sometimes the things they say come true?" The Prophet answered, "Yes, but the news they relate from the Jinn is mixed with hundreds of lies" (Hadith narrated by Bukhari from A'ishah).

The connection of fortune tellers with Jinn and devils is a strong bond. This bond, which has its foundation in evil, is an example of a symbolic agreement made to divert the faith and belief of humankind away from Allah and towards unseen forces as a refuge of help. They unceasingly whisper suggestions that bring about suspicion and doubt in humankind, which eventually brings them to the path of clear error.

The Prophet said, "Whoever goes to soothsayers and believes their words, he has disbelieved in that (the Qur'an) which was sent down to Muhammad" (Hadith narrated by Ahmad from Abu Hurairah).

It is imperative for Muslims, with Allah's help, to keep far away from shamans, soothsayers, fortune tellers, mediums, and clairvoyants. The aim of these people is to forge great lies in order to divert the *'aqidah* (belief) of the Muslim community away from the correct path.

Indeed, knowledge of life and death, happiness and grief, and difficulties and ease of all humankind is the domain of Allah alone. There is absolutely no one who can know the decrees of Allah and the lot that He appoints for each person, whether beneficial or detrimental. Humankind does not possess the capability, let alone the knowledge, to alter or determine the lot appointed to each one of them. These matters are included among affairs of the Unseen, which are hidden from the knowledge of humankind.

In the Qur'an, Allah has decreed:

"With Him (Allah) are the keys of the Unseen, the treasures that none knoweth but He..."
(Al-An'am: 59)

In a different verse, Allah states that only He is All-Knowing and fully-acquainted with knowledge of the Unseen, such as the time of Judgment Day, when rain will fall, what is in the womb of each female, the future gains of all humankind, and in which country each one of them will die:

"Verily, the knowledge of the Hour is with Allah (alone). It is He Who sends down rain, and He Who knows what is in the wombs. Nor does anyone know what it is that he will earn on the morrow. Nor does anyone know in what land he will die. Verily, with Allah is full knowledge and He is acquainted (with all things)."
(Luqman: 34)

"*Alif Lam Mim.* This is the Book; in it is guidance sure, without doubt, to those who fear Allah; who believe in the Unseen, are steadfast in prayer, and spend out of what We have provided for them."
(Al-Baqarah: 1-3)

The Prophet warned, "Whoever goes to fortune tellers and questions them about anything, his prayer will not be accepted for forty days" (Hadith narrated by Muslim from several wives of the Prophet).

> **"He (Allah alone) knows the Unseen, nor does He make anyone acquainted with His Secrets,—except a Messenger whom He has chosen..."**
> (Al-Jinn: 26-27)

Both the above-mentioned Quranic verse and Hadith clearly define the actual true connection between humankind and news of the Unseen. One aspect of modern-day society that is closely intertwined with many people's day-to-day lives is astrology through horoscopes and fortune-telling that supposedly reveals events or happenings of the Unseen. Both of these actions leave people greatly exposed to *shirk* (polytheism) and the setting up of partners with Allah, Most Powerful and Glorious.

A large number of humankind consider those persons who have knowledge and ability over aspects of the Unseen, who read the future of others and give helpful advice, as possessing a unique and extraordinary gift rarely found in average people. However, very few are aware that these practices are never devoid of elements of deceit, *shirk*, showing-off, and abundant lies and falsehoods.

The most worrying result stemming from these practitioners of astrology and fortune-telling is that they encourage and even teach others to take partners besides Allah.

They normally use tactics of attempting to brainwash people into believing that the knowledge or news that they pass on or teach others is purely inspiration or guidance given to them by God. Yet it is blatantly clear that they are not Messengers or Prophets of Allah, and therefore it is totally impossible that this comes from Allah. In fact, all knowledge and information of the Unseen they obtain is from beings other than Allah, i.e., Jinn and devils.

These practices are intended to make humankind gradually more dependent on beings other than Allah, which clearly constitutes *kufr* (unbelief).

Islam has never forbidden its followers from visiting those who have the ability and expertise to diagnose and treat illnesses suffered by human beings. When the aim is viewed from the angle of benefit to humankind, efforts such as these are not in contradiction, provided humankind does not cease to put total trust in and surrender to Allah. Indeed, it is Allah who has sent down illness but He has also sent down its cure; some of which is known to humankind and some of which is yet unknown. However, Allah has never made something that is *haram* (forbidden) as a treatment or medicine to cure the diseases or disturbances that afflict humankind.

Based on this fact, there is no excuse for people to approach or, worse still, place their hopes in others who claim they have knowledge of the Unseen, in order to predict or ascertain illnesses or disturbances from which they may be suffering. It is highly probable that those who claim such will use the assistance of Jinn due to the desperation of those seeking their help. In reality, their actions constitute *kufr* (unbelief) and straying into error, both of which bring the anger of Allah.

The Prophet of God stated in the following narration:

"Whoever goes to an *'arraf* (fortune teller), his prayer will not be accepted for forty days." (Hadith narrated by Muslim.)

From Abu Hurairah, the Prophet Muhammad said:

"Whoever goes to a *kahin* (shaman) and accepts what he says, indeed he has disbelieved in that which was sent down to Muhammad" (Hadith narrated by Abu Dawud).

The Prophet Muhammad said, "Whoever goes to a soothsayer or fortune-teller and believes his words, surely he has rejected what was sent down to Muhammad" (issued by the four compilers of Hadith and authenticated by Al-Hakim).

From 'Imran bin Husain, "The Prophet said, 'They are not of us those who practice or seek *tatayyur* (determining bad omens based on signs of situations, birds and other things), those who read the future and those seek a reading from them, and those who practice magic and those who ask magic from them. Whoever goes to a fortune-teller and accepts what he says, indeed he has disbelieved in the revelation that was sent down to Muhammad" (Hadith narrated by Al-Bazzar with a *jayyid* (good) chain of narrators).

It may be clearly deduced from the above-mentioned Hadith of the Prophet that Islam completely forbids humankind from meeting with fortune tellers, practitioners of witchcraft and anyone similar who attempts to delve into areas of the Unseen. These Hadith clearly warn that whosoever practices these black arts becomes an unbeliever, as these practices are in opposition to the Message that was given to the Prophet Muhammad.

Unbelief of those who practice magic

The Prophet of Allah has prohibited his followers from approaching clairvoyants and fortune tellers, because they come under the category of people who spread lies and deceit among humankind.

The Prophet's Hadiths clearly indicate the proof that shamans and fortune tellers are considered unbelievers, as they claim to have the ability to know the mysterious affairs of the Unseen of which the rest of humanity is ignorant. However, one should be aware that the only way they may hear something about the Unseen is through companionship or honoring and worshipping the Jinn and devils in order to obtain their aid and assistance. This situation clearly constitutes unbelief and *shirk* (setting up of partners) to Allah.

Those who embark upon the study of magic in effect only learn things that actually bring harm upon themselves and do not benefit them even in the slightest.

Generally, *shirk* is the action of equating something with Allah in regard to principles that are regarded as the rights of Allah, such as acts of worship, granting benefit or sending harm, seeking help and protection, etc.

There are many people who perhaps become amazed when they witness an unusual or extraordinary event, so much so that they deem it a miracle. In fact, miracles are special abilities and happenings that are solely sent to Prophets and Messengers as evidence of the truth they bring. Witchcraft, on the other hand, consists of harmful deeds that bring pain and suffering or even the performing of extraordinary actions with the assistance of unseen beings, particularly Jinn.

The necessary treatment to be administered to victims of disturbance by Jinn and devils normally consists of the recitation of verses from the Qur'an, or du'as of protection that are authenticated by the Sunnah of Prophet Muhammad. Through these types of righteous acts people may protect themselves and others from the harmful effects of Jinn interference such as possession, magic spells and severe mental disturbance.

There are a number of confusing issues surrounding the relationship of Jinn and devils that frequently arise.

It is a fact that the issuing of the *ruh* (spirit) that is breathed into the human body before birth comes under the domain of the Unseen, the sole truth of which is known to Allah alone. Therefore, on the occasion the Prophet Muhammad was questioned regarding the *ruh*, Allah revealed the following for him to answer,

"They ask thee concerning the Spirit. Say: 'The Spirit is of the command of my Lord: of knowledge it is only a little that is communicated to you, (O men!)'"
(Al-Isra':85)

There is no verse or proof, either in the Qur'an or Sunnah, indicating that the spirit that has left the lifeless body is able to materialize in the identical form as the deceased person in life, nor can it enter the body of someone else. It is solely Jinn and devils who have the power to change form by the permission of Allah.

In addition to this, there is a prevailing notion that human beings do not have the power to affect or harm Jinn who become visible. This opinion is in contradiction with various sources proving that devils who materialize and appear in different forms may be harmed or even killed. In an incident related by Abu Sa'id Al-Khudri, one of the Prophet's Companions killed a snake who bit another Companion.

When the incident was related to the Prophet, he said, "In this city of Medina, there are Jinn who have entered Islam. Therefore if any of you see one of them, repel it and continue to do so for up to three days. If it has not left by then, kill it for it is a devil" (Hadith narrated by Muslim).

In this narration, it is clear that devils and Jinn who appear in different forms can be harmed or even killed, as was done by one of the Companions of the Prophet.

Another mistaken impression among society in general is that Jinn and devils know everything about the Unseen, as if their knowledge regarding affairs that are veiled from human sight or understanding is the same as that which is known to Allah.

This issue is not confined to this level; it crosses beyond these boundaries to the point where it has become almost a general belief in society that whatever concerns people in the way of unseen issues beyond human control, such as matters of *rizq* (livelihood) or marriage, they will seek shamans or practitioners of black arts as a means of solution to these issues. Eventually, their faith in Allah's power no longer remains and becomes replaced with reliance on the shaman's power, which undoubtedly involves the interference of Jinn and devils.

In reality, Jinn in many aspects are the same as human beings and particularly with regard to issues of the Unseen. However, on account of the inborn advantages Jinn and devils possess, such as the ability to change form and move at amazing speed, they take advantage of these abilities to dazzle and sway human beings to the point where they become reliant on them and seek their help.

The Jinn themselves have been narrated in the Qur'an as admitting to their lack of knowledge of the Unseen:

"And we understand not whether ill is intended to those on earth, or whether

**their Lord (really) intends to guide them
to right conduct."**
(Al-Jinn: 10)

Allah has also demonstrated to humankind
the lacking of Jinn and devils in knowledge of
affairs of the Unseen, as illustrated in the well-
known story surrounding the death of Prophet
Sulaiman:

**"Then, when We decreed (Solomon's)
death, nothing showed them his death
except a little worm of the earth, which
kept (slowly) gnawing away at his staff: so
that when he fell down, the Jinn saw plainly
that if they had known the Unseen, they
would not have tarried in the humiliating
punishment (of their task)."**
(Saba': 14)

Furthermore, there are many other confused
or misguided perceptions pertaining to the world
of Jinn mistakenly adopted by humankind. One
very popular custom is the use of talismans or
amulets.

Nowadays, if we discuss the ways to protect
ourselves or avoid the harmful effects of magic or
disturbance by Jinn and devils, almost all religions

and beliefs contain their own particular methods to effect this aim. Despite this, however, these acts carry the perilous risk of bringing people to misguidance. This is due to the use amulets, talismans, protective charms hung on walls, or objects of various other names that people believe can afford them protection against evil. These are all forms of *shirk* (polytheism) about which the Prophet Muhammad has warned, "Whoever wears (or hangs) a talisman has committed *shirk*" (Hadith narrated by Ahmad).

It should always be borne in mind that Allah is the God who has created everything that exists in the universe. Indeed it is Allah alone who is All-Knowing about the true nature of all beings He has created. Therefore the actions and beliefs of a section of humankind who put their trust in the power of devils and Jinn, or even amulets and talismans to protect them from danger are customs that deviate in the extreme from the truth.

CHAPTER 4: MYSTERIOUS PHENOMENA OF THE UNSEEN WORLD

In this chapter, we will commence a step-by-step exploration into the realm of mystery: the secret world. This is a extremely strange world about which very little is known to humankind.

It is a dimension that is highly vague and abstract to the majority of people. It is a realm that cannot be simply defined to a particular space or time. This is the true state of the unseen world.

This is the world of Jinn. It is not a fairytale or fable of the people from ancient times. If we look into how and what is their form of existence, we will find that Jinn are not very different to humankind in various aspects.

In the same manner as the norms covering human life and routine, Jinn also have families, descendants, leadership, and governments. They have their own rulers and administrations. They are highly intelligent to the level of genius, in addition to possessing power and strength hundreds of times greater than that of humankind.

It is an indisputable fact that Jinn are one of the most impressive and highly developed beings created by Allah, compared to others of His creation found on the face of the earth.

If we translate this into a simple analogy, the intelligence of Jinn far exceeds that of the most advanced computer on earth, their ability to move is much faster than any jet aircraft that has ever been developed, whereas their ability to perform tasks is much more efficient and quicker than any sophisticated machine produced by human technology.

If, for instance, at a certain moment someone unintentionally disturbed them, they would not ignore or overlook it. Whatever action taken by people to hide themselves or flee from them would be in vain because Jinn possess vision that can see over distances of thousands of kilometers.

As we all know very well, the human experience is to be born on this earth, live between sixty and seventy years in normal cases, and then die. This process will continue uninterrupted until the Day of Judgment. Whenever the appointed time of death has come, there is no one nor thing that can escape this reality, including animals, plant life, and micro-organisms invisible to the naked eye.

The situation is quite different in the world of Jinn, as they are bestowed with long life. Among the Jinn born in this world—whether they were born in the time of Prophet Adam or our present time—almost a half of their numbers will be alive until the Day of Judgment.

Allah has permitted these beings to live side-by-side with humankind on this earth, and they are found wherever human beings may be: in the house, bedroom, office, or car; by the seashore or atop the peak of a high mountain. Anywhere human beings are found, they are very near but restricted from being seen by the naked human eye.

Allah declares in the Qur'an:

"I have only created Jinn and men that they may worship me."
(Adh-Dhariyat: 56)

The true reason behind the creation of Jinn—as well as humankind—who have been blessed with the capabilities of reason and emotion is to obey the divine command to worship Allah through obligatory acts of righteousness and devote themselves completely as true slaves to Him.

The creation of the first Jinn took place a very long time before the creation of humankind. At the time of his coming into existence, the Jinn was physically complete, intelligent, and very handsome. He lived in the garden of paradise surrounded by its intense beauty that dazzled and captivated the eye.

Unexpectedly, an event took place that marked the first point in history of the contact between humankind and Jinn. For no apparent reason, arrogance and pride due to his handsome form and special status began to enter the Jinn's heart until eventually it took him over completely and became a part of his nature.

His character then became full of hatred and treachery by which he attempted to influence the Angels into disobeying Allah. In short, this Jinn was the first being to commit sin, one which will not be forgiven even to the Day of Judgment. Since the very beginning of the creation of his race, he has carried this burden of great sin. Allah removed him from a special position in Paradise, along with all the blessings He bestowed on him.

All of this honor disappeared in a moment when he was banished from Paradise and sent down to earth.

In addition to the story mentioned above that is generally known, there is another belief in relation to the Jinn that Allah had previously ordered them to administer and rule the whole world. Despite this, they betrayed His command and created discord and destruction, as well as the mutual slaying of each other. In the end, God dispatched another group of Jinn from Paradise led by Angels to wipe out the Jinn who created discord and destruction on earth. They were finally defeated, but those who managed to survive moved to a different place on earth. The places they vacated were taken over by the Jinn from Paradise, who have remained there till this very day.

With Allah's permission, Jinn have the power to take over the world

If Allah permitted it to happen, Jinn have the capability and power to control or even colonize the whole world, on account of the various different innate advantages and special abilities they possess. They could achieve this end without the need of a million-strong army, nor the necessity of any weapons of mass destruction.

When viewed from the parameters of strength and abilities, those possessed by humankind are far removed and greatly restricted compared to those of Jinn in every respect. Logically, humankind would not have any other choice but to follow and obey, as well as become "errand boy" to the commands of the Jinn. Without doubt, no one would have the capability to prevent them from causing chaos throughout the whole world and its inhabitants. The power and terror of a Jinn governance could never witness anything equal to it up to the Day of Judgment.

Their extreme strength and power goes beyond the level that could be challenged, no matter what preparations humankind could muster up in the way of sophisticated technology. Every kind of endeavor and effort in the mobilization of all forces and power under humankind's possession, from every direction and corner of the earth, to face the power and might of the Jinn would be in vain and to the detriment of humankind, because they are too feeble to stand up to the superior abilities that Allah has bestowed on the Jinn.

The only surety is that the Jinn could very simply destroy humankind and obliterate them from the face of the earth in the blink of an eye.

There is a reason why humankind should be eternally grateful to Allah for his blessings and care. Due to His wish to shower mercy on and protect His slaves among humankind, He has decreed that from all His creation it is humankind that should shoulder the responsibility to make the earth prosper and be under man's control until the Day of Judgment.

One question rarely considered is exactly how large is the population of Jinn in the world? In actual fact, there are roughly nine times more Jinn on earth than that of the whole of humankind. If we consider that the current population of humankind is approximately 6 billion, this puts the population of Jinn at a staggering 54 billion!

Regardless of this number, if Allah permitted the situation to happen it would only take one individual from the Jinn—at most two or three—to create a situation of disturbance or chaos all over the world with great ease. A situation like this on earth would put everything under the Jinn's control.

Despite this, the remarkable advantage and power of 54 billion Jinn in the world is no match for the power, dominance, and greatness of Allah. Not just the Jinn; even if the whole of the combined forces of Jinn and devils on earth were gathered together, they would still be subject to the authority of Allah.

All this should serve to remind humanity and make them always aware that they have no place of refuge to seek protection except with Allah, and they must continually be grateful and glorify Him as the Lord Most High.

If Allah removed His protection and mercy from humankind, it would be certain that there would never be any opportunity to enjoy the blessings and happiness of a peaceful life as many experience today. On the contrary, humankind as a whole would be subject to an environment of never-ending terror and anxiety. We only need to imagine the power and frightening ability of only one individual from the Jinn unleashing chaos and decimation on the whole of humanity.

If we bring up the subject of Jinn and the unseen world, the usual attitude among people is that some believe they exist, whereas others do not and may even feel no sense of worry or anxiety about the evil effects and power of Jinn.

This should come as no surprise because such people may have never had knowledge or experience of any episode that involves these beings. As for those who are aware of the danger and deceit of Jinn and devils and have personal experience of the existence of Jinn and their destructive effect and interference upon humankind, it is certain that they will always adopt a cautious and wary attitude towards them.

Usually, the faces and physical forms of these creatures are not extremely horrifying and hideous as one might imagine. However, it should always be borne in mind that at any time they can completely change the form of their faces into any shape they desire, even one that a human would find truly terrifying.

If one of these creatures should suddenly manifest its face in a form that is highly gruesome and nightmarish, it would not be improbable that the person witnessing this could go insane or suddenly fall sick in such a manner that would be difficult to cure, or in more critical cases, die of shock.

They have also been given the ability to change the appearance and size of their bodies to any form they please. It is possible for them to reduce themselves minutely to the size of a particle or bacteria, or the height of six inches or ten feet. They can even reach eighty feet in height.

Although this may be the case, they are usually consistent to the habit of manifesting in the forms of a black dog, a black snake, or a black cat. It is believed that their preference for the color black is because it absorbs heat commensurate to the necessary temperature vital for them to survive. Therefore it is not unusual for them to select places to live which are dark. They cannot stand living in the hot sun. Generally they are inactive during day time.

The most disturbing aspect of their ability to transform their shapes and appearance is the example of being able to appear in a form that resembles an individual human being in precisely every way.

In such a situation where it transforms itself physically into an exact copy of a human being and then, for instance, enters that person's house when he or she is not home, the spouse, children, other family members or anyone else present in the house at that time would not notice any difference between the transformed Jinn and the actual human individual.

The confusion of this situation is contributed to even more due to the Jinn's complete transformation into an exact replica of the human individual down to the very last trait and physical detail, even copying the person's body smell.

Yet more unfortunate is that the individual's husband or wife will never suspect that the person who has entered the house is in fact a Jinn in disguise, because of the manner in which it imitates the human individual completely, including his or her character, voice, and behavior.

Even if there are people who dispute the fact that every individual person's voice can vary, nevertheless Jinn have been bestowed with the ability to change their voices to any tone and range they desire, from a voice that terrifies ranging to a voice that is extremely melodious and sweet. If a Jinn should sing a song, the listener would be truly touched and captivated by the sweetness of its voice.

In certain situations, a Jinn can transfer its beautiful voice to anyone who desires to make use of it. The individual who gains this kind of voice will feel great delight as if he or she were in a dream-like state.

Due to this ability of the Jinn, cases are sometimes heard of people who honor and worship Jinn solely to have a voice that is sweet and melodious.

What is perhaps more worrying and difficult for the rational mind to absorb is the ability of Jinn to communicate via a medium of communication such as a telephone in the same way as humankind. They are able to talk to human beings through the use of these objects. Jinn also possess the added advantage of being able to communicate in any language that exists in the world.

In any civilized society of humankind in this age, one of the main issues that has become the subject of ordinary people's conversation is the sophistication of the latest technological gadgets or equipment, such as computers, jet passenger airplanes, robots, and numerous other innovative inventions brought about through previously applied research and development.

Yet no matter how amazed humankind may feel about the current-day sophisticated technology, when compared to the level of sophistication that the technology of the Jinn has attained, it is backward and underdeveloped. The amazing power and ability possessed by the beings of the unseen world existed naturally from the moment they opened their eyes for the first time.

If they wish to perform or carry out anything they desire, they have no need to invent or produce something towards that aim. To clarify by way of comparison, they are able to dive to the depths of the Pacific Ocean in a few seconds; they can fly from America to Japan in the blink of an eye. If they wanted to build the tallest skyscraper in the world, they could very simply complete the project in a matter of seconds.

These comparisons previously mentioned are not amazing and wonderful stories like *Superman*. They are the reality behind the existence of Jinn who live on earth alongside humankind. These actual descriptions have all come about as a result of their creation.

With regard to their sense of humor, Jinn continually delight in amusing themselves with and playing practical jokes on humankind.

However, the disturbing aspect of their ways of joking or amusement is that they are totally unacceptable to human social norms as they contain elements of cruelty and barbarism, despite being viewed among the Jinn as being mere jokes.

This can be compared to the example of when a small child is busy playing with a kitten. Unexpectedly, the child puts the kitten inside a glass jar and then closes the lid. Not long after, the kitten suffocates to death. This illustration is a similar example of the Jinn sense of humor. In the same simple way, it demonstrates how easy it is for them to play practical jokes that may lead to tragedy.

Imagine when a mosquito or ant bites your arm. On account of the pain, you strike the creature without a second thought or any sense of regret. The same analogy may be applied to the Jinn. They feel no sense of guilt or regret for their actions, even if those actions lead to the death of a human being.

Generally, the Jinn are classified into two groups. The first group consists of those who are popularly known as Jinn, whereas the second group consists of those called devils, demons, or satans. The primary thing that differentiates one group from the other is whether they follow of one of the religions that exist in the world. The group of Jinn consists of those who possess beliefs and follow a particular religion. The group of devils, demons, or satans consists of those who do not follow any form of religion.

As a comparative example of the deviousness of their behavior and character, it is said that the most cowardly Jinn individual in the world of Jinn is equal to the most violent human being on the face of the earth. Yet it should always be borne in mind that devils are a type of Jinn who are far more violent, evil, dangerous, and harmful to humankind. Satan is the symbol that epitomizes evil and immorality in this world; Satan is not solely the enemy of humankind, but also the arch-enemy of everything good and pure in this world.

This is in line with a universal fact that ever since the first pages of history between Satan and humankind were written, it has been his vow to misguide the children of Adam by any means possible until the Day of Judgment.

Hysteria

Hysteria is a symptom of emotional disturbance of which most people may have some knowledge. When "hysteria" is mentioned, it usually brings to mind a scene of an individual or group screaming without apparent reason, becoming delirious, and finally fainting. It would not be extreme to say that most cases that come to our ears pertaining to hysteria follow the previously mentioned example. Usually it is mainly women who are prone to sudden or unexpected attacks of hysteria. The first symptoms observed prior to an attack are acute feelings of stress and anxiety, followed by a sudden change in behavior resulting in wild and uncontrollable outbursts.

The word "hysteria" is a term that has become a part of the history of human society now for the past thousands of years. Based on historical evidence, hysteria has been recorded in manuscripts dating back to the civilization of Ancient Egypt. The incident of hysteria as is known to society today occurred in various forms throughout history within the cultural context and medical perspective of the respective eras.

From the etymological viewpoint, the word "hysteria" comes from the Greek word *hysterikos* meaning "womb." The Greek physician Hippocrates believed that hysteria was a condition that affected women because, according to his knowledge, the womb was in continual movement throughout the woman's body and not fixed in one place.

In the subject of psychology, "mass hysteria" is the name given to the phenomenon in which the symptoms of hysteria occur among more than one person. The symptoms of hysteria usually appear in one individual, and then other individuals in the vicinity of the first suddenly develop similar symptoms. This phenomenon of mass hysteria is an example among the symptoms of psychoses such as paranoia and delusion that can transfer from one individual to another.

Modern-day psychologists are of the opinion that hysteria is normally caused by stress. Although hysteria is more synonymous with the world of medicine and is recognized as a medical term, this is due to usually being referred to as an illness or symptom connected to disturbances of the nervous system that cause sensory and motor activity dysfunction or failure. However, it is not understood and is highly puzzling as to why in certain cases the particular actions or behavior of the affected person goes way beyond the boundaries of her limitations.

Certain aspects cannot be explained from a rational perspective. In certain circumstances when an individual is afflicted by a sudden attack of hysteria, she may be able to talk in many different languages that she has never previously studied. More puzzling than this, she may even talk in old or ancient languages that are nowadays only understood by an exclusive group of linguistic experts.

In addition to the ability to speak in various foreign languages, another normal observation in certain individuals undergoing attacks of hysteria is abnormally higher degrees of physical strength when compared to the average person. In certain situations such as these, a small young female may suddenly develop the strength equal to ten strong and fit adult males.

We shall now look at certain interesting observations concluded by the author through his own personal experiences in connection with the unseen world of Jinn.

Hysteria is an aggressive attack perpetrated by Jinn who enter the body and mind of human beings causing them to suddenly develop amazing strength of impossible and unbelievable proportions.

Once Jinn successfully slip inside the body and mind of human beings, it is extremely hard to expel them. It is only Allah, All-Knowing, who knows the true reason why they refuse to leave the body and why their exorcism is such a difficult process.

Efforts to remove or exorcise a Jinn that has entered and possessed an individual's body are usually very time consuming. The surface of the human skin is an area that is highly exposed to Jinn entering the body prior to controlling the mind and personality of the individual. It is quite possible that the unusual sensation of a very fine, short wave experienced in the brain of a person undergoing an attack of hysteria will bear a close connection with the presence of a supernatural being inside the body.

Someone afflicted by hysteria could be considered very fortunate when undergoing treatment to expel a Jinn from controlling their body and mind if it were exorcised in a short period of time by a person who understands the problem and knows something about Jinn and the unseen world. As for those practitioners of hidden arts connected to the Jinn world, their preferred methods are the use of specific spiritual procedures, incantations, or even verses of the Qur'an as ways to overcome disturbances caused by these creatures.

Nevertheless, if the Jinn possessing certain individuals suffering from attacks of hysteria are allowed to control the body and mind for a considerable period of time, eventually this will aggravate the situation whereby these individuals will remain in a constant state of suffering and misery until it becomes extremely difficult to treat them. If left to continue, the long-term situation will result in mental illness or insanity.

In most cases observed, those persons possessed by Jinn do not usually know or may even be totally unaware of when and how the Jinn began to control them. More worrying that this is the possibility of death occurring if treatment to seek a cure for the victim is delayed. No one should underestimate interference or attacks of the Jinn nor regard them as superficial. Jinn should never be taken lightly or made the objects of ridicule and amusement.

For example in the Thai film entitled *Nang Nak,* the storyline is about a Jinn who takes on human form. This is not impossible because we know that they can materialize in almost any shape. This is actually one of the methods of Jinn interference that leave humankind totally unaware when it takes place.

However, the notable scene in the film where the Jinn is seen in a physical form carrying out violent attacks is quite nonsensical and improbable. If such a situation does ever occur, it is extremely rare and is only perpetrated by extremely fierce Jinn.

There may be perhaps significant numbers among us who have seen the well-known horror film made in Hollywood in 1973 called *The Exorcist.* It was written by William Peter Blatty and featured popular actors of the time such as Linda Blair, Peter Miller and others.

Taking a closer look at this film, the author of this book believes that many practitioners of unseen arts who have watched it will recognize that besides being a shocking and terrifying film, it also contains elements that are factual and could possibly take place.

The storyline of the film revolves around an unclear phenomenon that is affecting a young girl living in an American city. It comes to light that she is possessed by an evil presence, so an expert in expelling evil beings from a person's body or an *exorcist* (after which the film is named) is called in to save her from the attacks and interference that result from this possession.

Among the scenes that mystify and bring many questions to mind is one whereby the young girl suddenly becomes full of power and develops extraordinary physical strength. Even more mesmerizing is the scene where she is floating in the air without any apparent reason. If we look at it from the aspect of a film critic, it is scenes such as these that act as the main force to hold the viewer's attention, especially those viewers who are interested in the occult.

Whatever the case may be, nevertheless it is an example of a film that exploits the true reality of this phenomenon regarding the situation and experiences undergone by a person under the influence of Jinn.

Therefore, it came as no surprise that much acclaim and many accolades were received by the film's director, William Freidkin.

All aspects of the film were portrayed in a completely accurate manner and according to a correct representation. According to those who have studied the world of Jinn, the director produced a film replete with realistic elements and facts that did not go beyond the limits in portraying the actual circumstances.

The point being stressed here is that action of a highly mesmerizing nature, such as the young girl floating in air, is a representation of the true phenomena that affect a person possessed by Jinn. It should be added that under certain circumstances, it is not impossible to move about high in the sky and with speed.

In addition, there was also another significant scene in the film where the assistant of the priest (the exorcist) suddenly breaks into a fit of rage when he witnesses the young girl attempting to kill the priest. Therefore, he in turn steps in and tries to strangle her.

This leads to the Jinn inside the young girl leaving her body all of a sudden and possessing his body instead. The Jinn gradually takes control of him until it results in tragedy, whereby the Jinn forces him out of a window to fall to his death.

If such a scene occurred in a real-life situation, it would be necessary for one attempting to communicate with an individual under the possession of a Jinn to take certain preventative measures. One must be patient and take each step very carefully, because at that actual moment one is no longer facing a human being but the Jinn who has taken control of his or her body.

In this tense situation, it is imperative to remember that communication with them must be carried out in a slow and pleasant manner because Jinn are beings who are uncouth, hot-tempered, and known to react violently towards those who raise their voices. One must never slap or provoke someone possessed by Jinn, because such actions will provoke greater and even more dangerous enmity from them.

It would only be a matter of time before they seek revenge. This revenge could come instantly, or after a month, a year or even many years later when the human being has long since forgotten the incident. Jinn, however, do not forget like humankind. They always remember any action that has been done against them.

More disturbing than this, they do not always carry out retribution against the actual person to whom they bear a grudge. They may select a member of his family as the object of revenge, irrespective of how terrifying or unjust this course of action may be.

If the process of communication opens with the Jinn possessing the body, it must always be borne in mind that not everything they utter is the truth. As has been previously mentioned, they are creatures who truly delight in tormenting and mocking humankind.

It is of great importance to point out that we must be able to ascertain by knowledge and without a shadow of doubt the difference between cases where an individual is mentally ill and where one is possessed by a Jinn. This is because treatment of these two types of individuals takes on vastly different forms.

In addition, it is imperative to differentiate in order to prevent a much worse situation afflicting the person possessed by a Jinn. Victims of hysteria are at risk of become mentally unbalanced if the first steps of treatment are not carried out in a correct manner. It is most unfortunate that the majority of hysteria victims are mistakenly admitted to mental hospitals. While acknowledging that victims of genuine attacks and interference by Jinn can become insane, usually this occurs in more less thirty to forty percent of cases, or maybe more.

There are also cases whereby certain numbers of hysteria victims, who, after being admitted to mental hospitals, were given electric shock therapy (ECT) to stimulate the brain, which produced no positive effects. However, following treatment by spiritual practitioners who managed to exorcise the Jinn from their bodies, they made a complete recovery.

From one aspect, despite the special ability of those experts who study the unseen world in that they are able to treat victims of Jinn attacks and hysteria, they also represent those individuals who are at the highest risk of exposure to attack by unseen beings. Therefore it is usual for them to take necessary precautions to prevent any such occurrences from happening and protect themselves.

One of the additional reasons why Jinn enter the human body is anger towards the human victim, based on several reasons that may be known or unknown to the victim.

A common example is when someone pours boiling water in places such as drains or toilets, causing death among the Jinn. Any action that results in the death of even one Jinn will undoubtedly provoke its companions to seek revenge. It is not generally known, but this is one of the main reasons that spur Jinn on into interfering with humankind.

Whenever we study the causes of many cases of hysteria, we find that in general women form the majority of victims. This is on account of a number of physical factors such as being softer emotionally when compared to men and also due to menstruation. Basically, Jinn truly like the taste of blood, and they are very fond of menstrual blood. Another cause is due to male Jinn falling in love with these women.

However, it should be borne in mind that sometimes they will interfere with human beings for no apparent reason. If this takes place, the sole prime factor usually at the root of the cause is the emotional and mental state of the individual they select, which facilitates their entry into the body and subsequent disturbance of the individual.

When human beings find themselves in situations of emotional instability, such as pressure, stress, and emotional turmoil, e.g., during moments of extreme anger, fear, anxiety, weakness, acute depression, or a host of other forms of unstable emotions and uncertain mental state, they are inadvertently giving the green light and an indication of their Achilles' heel for the Jinn to observe and attack.

In fact, the vast majority of people are not conscious of the fact that Jinn may be present inside their bodies.

The moment people lose their temper or fly into a rage, suddenly and immediately they become full of energy, strong and fierce. They cannot think rationally. More seriously, they are a danger to others and especially those in close proximity. They are quite capable of committing murder at any time, because during those periods they are being controlled by Jinn.

In addition, at the time people are asleep, Jinn may enter their bodies without any difficulty.

It would not be extreme to say that the reason certain individuals who are in a deep state of sleep suddenly get up and sleep-walk is because they are being guided by Jinn.

In moderate cases many people, including perhaps the reader, may have felt as if there is a shape or perhaps even a shadow pressing down on them while they are asleep. However, when they open their eyes they cannot see anything around them. This is another manifestation of Jinn disturbing or attacking us.

It cannot be stressed enough that the human body is highly exposed to attack and interference by supernatural creatures. For instance, during confrontations that take place between Jinn themselves, those who are weak or unable to stand up to other Jinn will use a human body as a hiding place. They consider the human body as one of the safest places to conceal themselves.

Sexual intercourse with Jinn

It has been said that "love is blind." Perhaps this is no doubt true when applied to human beings. However, what would we think if someone known to us fell in love with another human being who was actually from the Jinn? It might sound unlikely, but it does take place.

Whatever the case, whether it is a male Jinn who falls in love with a human female or a female Jinn falling in love with a human male, both combinations indicate unfavorable situations for human beings. They represent the first signs of serious trouble for the humans involved.

Although the term "falling in love" is used, in fact the situation is vastly different from two human beings falling in love with each other. This is because Jinn will start to disturb the person it loves by varying methods, the most popular of which is entering and possessing the human's body.

More far-reaching than this, love of this kind does not stop at disturbing the person who has become the object of the Jinn's affections. The Jinn will attempt to have sexual intercourse with the person either physically or spiritually. Unfortunately, they usually do this without the consent of the human in question.

In many mysterious cases of this kind, women who have become victims of rape by Jinn have only experienced the assault spiritually. It is as if the sexual act is taking place but the perpetrator cannot be seen through the victim's eyes.

The harm that comes about from this kind of Jinn disturbance can result in a much worse situation taking place. For instance, in addition to the spiritual interference when they are infatuated with human beings, they can also cause division between husband and wife. A couple who have been married for a long time and who have passed through many happy experiences together can gradually and unconsciously begin to grow apart.

In cases where a male Jinn becomes infatuated or falls in love with a human female, he will disturb her in ways such as trying to influence her by whispering seductive suggestions inside her very being. The form of these suggestions will be gentle, touching, attractive, and no less than arousing until gradually they have a disturbing effect on her feelings, emotions, and mind.

If such a situation results, it is not unusual for a married woman to leave her husband. Aside from this, the situation may become more desperate if the Jinn begins to disturb or attack the husband, either in the same manner as it did to his wife or in a much more dangerous way by driving him insane or killing him through the sudden development of a mysterious illness.

The woman whom the Jinn has succeeded in influencing to leave her husband will only begin to realize with a clear mind the seriousness of her actions after the Jinn has left her. Almost all individuals who were victims of disturbances through suggestions and domination by the Jinn were previously unaware of the actions that resulted in the breakdown of their marriages. Everything they did was not based on their own desires or wishes, but on account of the influence of the Jinn.

If we closely examine the forms of disturbance that are undergone by women who have become the object of Jinn affections, among them is experiencing the sensation of sexual intercourse taking place in dreams with a person who cannot be seen. In realistic terms the experience is the same in every way. For instance, feeling arousal that brings the same effects as one feels when awake. This disturbance is not just undergone mentally, but it is also a physical experience that stimulates the psychology and physiology of the victim. For this reason, interference such as this can eventually result in orgasm.

Among the general symptoms felt as a result of this kind of Jinn disturbance is an extraordinary feeling of tiredness after the sexual act has taken place. In more serious situations, the Jinn may carry out the sexual attack several times in one night.

The following verse is found in the Bible:

"More and more people were born, until finally they spread all over the earth. Some of their daughters were so beautiful that supernatural beings came down and married the ones they wanted, Then the Lord said, 'I won't let my life-giving breath remain in anyone forever. No one will live more than one hundred twenty years.' The children of the supernatural beings who had married these women became famous heroes and warriors. They were called Nephilim and lived on the earth at that time and even later."
(Genesis 6:1–4, Contemporary English Version, American Bible Society, 1996).

Obviously, this relationship is made up of two beings that are completely different in all aspects, but this does not exclude them from the possibility of pregnancy resulting. A number of true incidents have occurred that are extremely difficult to explain from the perspective of medicine, such as the embryo or fetus inside a pregnant woman suddenly disappearing without trace. Children usually born of a paranormal relationship are raised in the world of Jinn.

The occurrence of such a relationship must seem frightening and illogical to us whereby the coming together of two completely different beings can produce a tangible effect on a human being physically. Despite the many theories and explanations that abound by experts attempting to elucidate the phenomena, the actual fact is that it is a result of actions perpetrated by unseen beings.

Jinn desire that their half-human children be raised in their world. Under these circumstances, these children will develop precisely like them and live their whole lives in the unseen world.

The relationship between a mother and child is an extremely close connection typifying the maternal instinct that exists in the animal kingdom. The connection is much more significant among human beings. The mothering instinct to love her child is such an intrinsic part of a woman that it is a physical and mental impossibility for her to forget the offspring that she carried inside her for nine months. Another far-reaching result of this type of Jinn interference is that these mothers will never have the opportunity to be with their children in the real world, but only see them in dreams.

In a certain number of cases, this relationship will continue their whole lives. Moreover, it is not uncommon among the women who undergo this extraordinary phenomenon to suddenly develop the ability to treat various illnesses. What comes to mind when a situation like this occurs is that the cause is their children, who possess their mother's bodies while they carry out treatment and who also will give other forms of help to their mothers.

Although people in general might consider the abilities of these children extraordinary, nevertheless in their unseen world their childhood lasts for 500 years. The difference in life-span between Jinn and humankind is vast. Some Jinn live thousands of years, whereas others will live until the end of the world.

Despite this, there are still some children born of the union between the two rational species who possess the normal features of a human being, although many of them exhibit unique differences compared to other children of their respective ages. For instance, some of them without apparent reason have the unusual ability to treat illnesses; some possess strange powers, are highly intelligent and have other extraordinary characteristics and traits. They also embody the common personal traits of Jinn such as being powerful, harsh, and uncontrollable.

UFOs, the Bermuda Triangle and Jinn

Sightings of UFOs were first reported when the issue arose of a UFO falling to earth in Roswell, New Mexico, U.S., at the beginning of July 1947. This situation raised many assumptions that more or less tried to claim a close connection between the UFO and aliens from outer space.

In fact, a great deal of speculation has been generated from all over the world regarding UFOs. Among them were those ideas put forward by supporters of conspiracy theories that UFOs in space were closely connected to a military unit formed to exchange technology with an alien civilization. Others claimed that during the World War II, the Nazis had succeeded in producing airplanes that exactly resembled UFOs and that they were now hidden in underground military bases.

Furthermore, Zecharia Sitchin, a Jewish expert on ancient languages who had helped decipher the famous archeological discovery dating back to Sumerian history, the Dead Sea Scrolls, claimed that the species *Homo Sapiens,* or humankind, were the result of a genetic engineering experiment of the Anunnaki race from the planet Nibiru. However, David Icke, the famous British sports commentator turned new-age spiritualist, believes that aliens from outer space live in disguise amongst humankind and possess a hidden agenda that spells disaster for humankind.

From the viewpoint of psychoanalysis, there are certain speculative opinions that consider the phenomena of UFOs as not being real and only represent an occurrence based on a collective consciousness that connects one individual with different individuals throughout the world.

In fact, there are many other assumptions and interpretations coming from many other quarters and individuals who have researched into UFOs that are far too numerous to be documented here. The point that must be stressed here is that it would not be extreme to say that UFOs represent a version of supernatural beings in a more modern guise parallel to the development of today's contemporary human civilization.

Nevertheless, the question still remains: from the myriad of opinions, which one is correct? It may well be acknowledged that the development of human technology has been truly rapid and sophisticated, but this is no reason to assume that with all these amazing human achievements of today humankind has attained the power to expose all the secrets of the unseen world that is veiled from the human eye. It should never be forgotten that the world we inhabit hides many thousands of mysteries that lie well beyond the capability of mere humankind to reveal, except by the permission of Allah:

"...He (Allah) knows what enters within the earth and what comes forth out of it, what comes down from heaven and what mounts up to it..."
(Al-Hadid: 4)

The information that humankind has obtained regarding the unseen world of Jinn is extremely limited. The sophisticated technology used by humankind to open up the world closed to the human eye is still far away from the reality of the situation. Due to this inadequacy, it is true to say that a great deal of misunderstanding has crept into human reason in clarifying and glimpsing the unseen world.

In this chapter we will focus on an important issue that is not classified as an unfathomable mystery, but one that captured the attention of the whole world not so long ago. Nowadays it may be assumed that almost everyone on earth has heard about the appearances of mysterious shapes moving at high speed through the sky causing surprise to those who witness them. These have been designated as unidentified flying objects, or UFOs. Some think they are beings from other worlds known as "aliens."

In reality, the manifestation of flying objects or alien spacecrafts are not an illusion or trick of the eyesight. They are phenomena that actually exist despite the inability of humankind to ascertain or assign them a correct definition.

According to a poll commissioned by the *Globe* in 1973, more than sixteen million Americans had themselves witnessed clear sightings of UFOs. Based on this poll, it was concluded that forty percent of citizens were of the opinion that the CIA was ineffective and unaware of secrets that were hidden from the American public.

From 1947 until 17 December 1969, the United States Air Force actively investigated reports and sightings of unidentified flying objects - UFOs, under a program called Project Blue Book. The project which was headquartered at Wright-Patterson AFB, was terminated in December of 1969 after 22 years.

On 20 July 1952, a group of people witnessed seven elongated spaceships that appeared above The White House in Washington. A fighter jet was dispatched to obstruct the objects. However, the fighter jet's controls were rendered inactive after a piercing beam of light was directed onto the jet by one of the spaceships. Immediately after this incident, all of the spaceship flew out of sight at an unusually fast speed.

At the same time, a team of intelligence agents from the United States Air Force prepared a special report to be presented to the top leadership of the Armed Forces regarding the issue of flying objects. A contributing factor to the credibility of the report was the opinions of trusted scientific experts and academicians. The following is an excerpt from the report:

"The studied phenomenon has been concluded to be one that is real and factual, and not based on supposition or imagination. What is certain, the appearance of capsule-shaped flying objects near earth approximately the size of our jets can in no way be denied based on the assumption that statements received by witnesses represent mistaken identification of phenomena from outer space or the passing of space debris such as meteors. These reports and also the speed of the said objects and the manner in which they maneuver indicate that they are carefully controlled, either manually, mechanically or by remote-control."

The attention of the world was diverted for a while and focused on this issue. Scientists, government agencies (such as the CIA and historians), and numerous individuals and organizations throughout the world endeavored with great enthusiasm to investigate the mystery behind the appearance of these flying objects.

The phenomena of UFOs and aliens had become an important issue that held society's attention in America since the start of the Cold War. The issue began with certain startling reports and statements from witnesses claiming to have actually seen them. The catalyst that triggered the issue to become the discussion point of the whole world was a number of photographs that captured images of these flying objects, although the authenticity of the pictures was greatly disputed. This issue was enough to spark the interest of other certain parties such as the U.S. Department of Defense and the mass media, in addition to the general public.

This was followed by eye-witness accounts and reports by individuals who had undergone bizarre experiences in connection with UFOs. This issue continued to fire the imagination of the world as a highly intriguing twentieth century mystery narrated on a massive scale, which still continues to this day. As a result of the effects of indoctrination and a mass media campaign in particular, little by little the people of the world began to believe in and become no less than obsessed with the subject of aliens and UFOs.

In addition to this, the United States government, not wanting to be left behind, took the initiative and launched a special worldwide "Project 1947" with the objective of documenting any information or facts relating to issues connected with aliens and UFOs.

This special project was pioneered and executed by a team of UFO experts, scientists, and other experts in various fields with the support of several official government agencies. One of the bodies involved in the research was the Center for UFO Studies (CUFOS), an international organization concentrating particularly on investigation and close study of the phenomenon of UFOs. In addition, many other efforts of similar research and investigation were carried out in various countries across the world.

At this point, we shall focus our attention on a number of amazing discoveries in connection with this subject.

Among the thousands of claims and statements of witnesses from all over the world who have seen UFOs, it was a pilot, Sub-Lieutenant J.E. Morgan in England, who was the first person ever to report an encounter with a flying object as it happened. In the same vein, the very first official report recorded about UFOs was during the Apollo 15 mission and was substantiated by photographic evidence taken through crypto space in NASA.

This event spurred on the Department of Defense (the Pentagon) to set up a special committee designated "Project Blue Book." This special committee was responsible for handling issues connected to flying saucers or unidentified objects from space, following the response received from the general public regarding the subject of UFOs increasingly flooding the mass media with the risk of a threat to peace resulting from panic and anxiety generated by a small group of individuals.

The first incident reported was that of an alien spacecraft that attacked an F-86 fighter jet. The F-86 was cruising at the rear of a flying saucer that was being observed by ground radar at an air base. The F-86 then changed course above a large field to pursue the spacecraft. Suddenly, the radar operator on the ground observed in a split second the flying saucer change course and make a beeline towards the American jet. The pilot received orders to take offensive action and without hesitation launched several attacks against the object. When the altercation died down, the only signal that could be observed on the radar screen was that of the flying s aucer.

The American radar operators immediately attempted to make contact with the flying saucer, which had already fled the scene, but all to no avail; no response was received. It seemed as if the fighter jet had disappeared inside the flying object. Without hesitation, the government mobilized its armed forces, and planes were dispatched to search for any part or debris of the F-86 that had vanished. However, no trace of the fighter jet was ever found. It was as if it had been a mirage.

The second incident involving a space ship resulted in the disappearance of twenty-six passengers aboard a troop transportation plane. The chronology of events leading up to the tragedy began with the appearance on a radar screen of a flying saucer moving at very fast speed. It was then seen changing course in the direction of the transportation plane. Before the radar operator even had the opportunity to warn the pilot, suddenly the radar screen displayed two objects merging into one in an instant. Then, in the blink of an eye, the remaining object vanished without trace from the field of radar.

In another situation in the southern United States, two policemen encountered a man and woman who appeared to be humanoid dressed in very strange garb. They stated to the officers,

"We have come from a different planet to help humankind."

In a similar case, Antonio Felas Bowas—an individual who was abducted by a flying saucer in 1958—claimed that his abductees aboard the saucer were humanoid aliens. When he attempted to flee from them, an alien the height of Antonio's shoulders grabbed him. He turned towards the alien and struggled, managing to push it back. However, three other aliens then captured him. They subsequently proceeded to perform unusual experiments on him. They took blood from him using a glass pipe connected to a glass container in a similar manner to the method of cupping practiced by Muslims in the Middle East.

In addition to these mysterious phenomena, many bodies and organizations have sprung up dedicated to searching for these flying objects that obsess and challenge the rational human mind. One such organization is Nikap, which is headed by the top-brass leadership of the United States Air Force. This issue has become the subject of much scrutiny and investigation. Incidentally, sometimes a UFO may also be referred to an OVNI, which is an acronym for unidentified flying object in Latin.

Despite the vast amount of empirical facts and data verifying the existence of flying saucers, there are still those who refuse to accept the phenomenon. They dismiss the issue as mere hallucination or delusion. Simultaneously, there are others who are convinced of their existence, although they claim these are aliens who have traveled to earth from other planets.

As for the phenomena of the Bermuda Triangle, countless interpretations and analyses have been put forward that illustrate a situation that is far from reality. For example, some believe that one reason for the phenomena is a giant wave resulting from an earthquake on the seabed. Others are of the supposition that ball lightning strikes planes crossing the Bermuda Triangle. However, it cannot be denied that some explanations are highly imaginative, such as those who claim the existence in the vicinity of a time portal that opens into different time dimensions.

Not long ago, attempts were made to take aerial images from the area above the Bermuda Triangle and the surrounding sectors using satellites and other sophisticated modern equipment. Mysteriously, the pictures sent back by satellite failed to appear on screen except one picture displaying an object that greatly resembled a land-mass. However, recording equipment located on a boat anchored at sea that was part of a scientific expedition near the Bermuda Triangle indicated that the presence of a land-mass in this area was an impossibility.

The man who discovered America, Christopher Columbus, safely crossed the area of the Bermuda Triangle in 1492. However, there is documented evidence stating he witnessed lights in the area, which bear the strong possibility of a connection with Jinn.

Speculation as to the possibility of other beings that travel around the area cannot be dismissed, because according to what was previously mentioned, oceans and seas are places occupied by Jinn and devils.

If we recap all that has been discussed up to this point, we have seen since the very beginning that Jinn have been brought into existence possessing extraordinary developed abilities with which humankind cannot compete. Included among those special powers is the ability to move at extremely fast speed—comparable to the speed of light—with or without a mode of transportation.

Based on the phenomena we have mentioned, the only reasonable conclusion we may reach at this point is that the phenomena of flying objects and aliens are real, but specifically their existence bears a very close connection to the unseen world—that is, Jinn.

Any discussion about the mysterious phenomena of UFOs and aliens cannot be complete without involving issues of science and religion. Among the theories expounded are those purporting the existence of alternative life-forms inhabiting other planets or dimensions of other worlds, beings that cannot be perceived by the senses.

Returning to our main point of discussion, Jinn are unique creatures possessing totally different characteristics compared to typical human ones. For example, basic elements such as oxygen and water are biological necessities for the survival of humankind on this earth. In contrast, reliance on elements such as those mentioned in no way bears any direct connection to the Jinn's survival. On account of their lack of dependence on elements that are vital to the survival of humankind, Jinn are not presented with any obstacles in inhabiting any other planet or dimension of any world that lies in the universe outside of earth.

Touching on the subject of principles and beliefs of humankind since time immemorial, basically there is no religion or form of belief that possesses any available information or physical proof pertaining to the presence of UFOs and alien beings on earth. The only exception is information commonly found in various religions or beliefs regarding the existence of unseen beings.

For almost the past thirty years, the assumed image and form of these phenomena that has been captured by the imagination is one that raises a feeling of anxiety and uncertainty among all levels of society in the world. To counter a possible threat from UFOs and alien creatures, certain parties have already embarked upon military programs that have been designed solely as precautionary steps to preempt a potential aggressive act by aliens. However, the only principle that could be wisely adopted in circumstances such as these would be to avoid wasting time and money in futile efforts to develop or modernize defense systems, such as the Star Wars project. It is a foregone conclusion that humankind would not have the power to defend itself against them.

Humankind should always be aware of its incapability to stand up to the power and advanced technology they possess. However, this does not mean the surrender and subjugation of earth without taking decisive action to find a solution to this dangerous issue. Without doubt, humankind would be in great need of correct advice and direction. Nevertheless, it would be pointless for humankind to make the mistake of wasting time, energy, and money amounting to billions of dollars in the pursuit of something that turns out to be ineffective. This same path of futility has been trodden—and is still—in the wide-scale propagation of Darwin's theory of evolution, which has effaced the last 140 years of learning in a particular field of biology with an unproven notion than has not resulted in any benefit to humankind.

Jinn as a whole do not die solely as a result of being shot or fired upon, even if the weapon is highly advanced and sophisticated, because they are unseen creatures. It is as if one fires a bullet at the wind; it produces no effect. The reality of the situation is that the only way to overcome them is by bringing ourselves closer to Allah.

Another interesting issue concerning UFOs and alien beings generally is widespread stories of people being abducted by aliens.

Included among incidents of this kind that have been reported publicly are people who maintain they can correctly identify individuals who claim to have been abducted by aliens. What comes as a surprise is that efforts to classify symptoms observed in abductees have revealed that a similar range of symptoms are displayed by victims undergoing attacks of hysteria.

Through close observation, they have discovered startling similarities between these two types of victims of very different conditions: aliens and hysteria. Both types of victims display memory recall that is vague and unclear. Alien abductees usually struggle to recall the series of events that appear detached from one another, such as mysterious lights, strange beings, futuristic medical examination equipment, and various other odd phenomena witnessed. More disturbing is the loss of memory regarding incidents during the abduction that were too horrific to recall.

There are also other similar symptoms shared by individuals of both conditions, such as extreme fear, panic, and paleness, which manifests in situations where they are in the vicinity of specific places or hear particular sounds, e.g., the sound of a helicopter that suddenly appears in the sky, although similar traumatic feelings may arise in different situations. In addition they may display anxious or distressed behavior when watching films or reading books or magazines that involve the subject of alien beings.

Disturbances at night indicate a situation where they are almost completely unprotected from Jinn, such as difficulty in sleeping and fear of the dark. Those disturbances usually also include nightmares in which they are being attacked by grotesque creatures of various forms, such as those with giant eyes and horns, resulting in them having continuous disturbed sleep for several nights. The morning after leaves them feeling insecure, confused, and nauseous, and their bodies feeling stiff or even devoid of sensation.

More disturbing are the effects that may actually manifest on their bodies. It is not uncommon to see these victims display cuts, bruises, and swelling in specific parts of their bodies, in addition to other symptoms of which the cause is unknown.

All of these symptoms mentioned are common indications of individuals who have undergone alien abduction or hysteria.

These signs may also be displayed by people who have been subjected to the type of Jinn interference whereby they are unable to be seen by others, which occurs particularly in forests or jungles. In short, these are all indicative of disturbances and attacks by supernatural beings.

Help from Jinn

The discussion up to this point has focused on the evil aspect and negative effects of disturbance and attack by Jinn. However, it is not unknown for Jinn to possess feelings of pity for humankind.

Jinn have been blessed with very long life and, as is common with all creatures, those who are older are wiser and more experienced than the younger ones among them. The same comparison may be applied when comparing the life-span of Jinn and humankind. On account of Allah bestowing them with much longer lives than human beings, it should come as no surprise that they possess the ability to treat illnesses that afflict humankind. If we look at it from a logical perspective, during the Jinn's life-span, which may reach thousands of years, the Jinn is able to gain a great deal more knowledge and learning than a human being can attain in a much shorter lifetime.

Those who engage in learning the black arts or even those whose bodies Jinn enter by chance may take advantage of the Jinn's assistance to seek an effective spell or cure for certain kinds of illnesses or diseases affecting people, especially those that doctors or physicians of conventional medicine cannot treat. Those who attain the knowledge or ability to treat unconventional illnesses through the aid of the Jinn that possess them usually find this special ability disappears when the Jinn leave their bodies. In fact, Jinn have been known to help human beings in different ways, such as in situations that occur unexpectedly and the persons concerned are in desperate need.

Nowadays when the subject of beautification arises, there are many people, particularly women, who desire to look more beautiful and younger. However, large amounts of money are required for this purpose through different processes. Some go for plastic surgery, and one of the latest and popular treatments in this field consists of Botox injections in the face to rejuvenate sagging facial tissue. Other individuals desperate to regain beauty and a younger look resort to less expensive treatment of a more traditional nature. By way of various rituals and superstitious practices, practitioners of spiritual and unseen power will carry out their own particular methods of treatment to attain the desired effect.

A number of specific methods are particularly popular in several Asian countries, one of which is where a small object made out of gold or precious stones is used to pierce the surface of the skin. The object, which is usually called *susuk* in Southeast Asia, is then inserted into the body following a particular method and ritual that is accompanied by the reciting of incantations. The spell results in the person looking more beautiful with a permanently younger look.

Despite this, the negative effects of this practice will become apparent later on in the lives of those who have these objects inside their bodies, particularly during the last few years prior to death. They will suffer from strange conditions such as the skin turning dark and extreme weakness of the whole body to the point where they have no strength even to move their fingers. When they reach this stage, the condition will have become so serious that they will be unable to recover. It may be concluded that although Jinn will never hesitate to offer aid to humankind, each and every form of assistance they furnish is paid in kind by much suffering on the human side.

Due to their special advantages and abilities, Jinn have the ability to alter the appearance and personality of a person to become much better than average, even strong and good-looking, but with it comes the danger of Jinn interference sooner or later.

Penetration into the world of Jinn is not an easy task. Usually the rituals performed among many practitioners of spiritual power are extremely difficult for ordinary people. Likewise, the same conditions apply to Jinn; only those who are truly capable and experienced possess the ability to enter the world of humankind.

It is ironic that Jinn also practice the recital of Quranic verses, incantations, and magic to penetrate into our world, in the same way human beings do to make their way into the Jinn's world. If all Jinn had been given the power to come and go without hindrance into the world of human beings, it is certain that humankind would have been enslaved by them. Nevertheless, it must be added that Jinn always respect human beings who hold fast to the commands and prohibitions of Allah and maintain a special relationship with Him, Most High.

Jinn residences

As has been clarified previously, despite the vast differences from many aspects regarding the creation of Jinn, the dissimilarities are not so apparent when compared to humankind from the aspects of daily life and basic necessities, such as the dwellings they inhabit.

In general, they live and occupy a particular space and area. As beings that possess feelings and emotions the same as humankind, they also have their own individual tastes and preferences in determining specific places they choose as residences.

As is common to people, some prefer to live by the sea, in cities, or places of rapid development.

Some have a preference for brick houses, whereas others prefer a house made of wood. The same applies to Jinn; their choices depend on their own particular likes and dislikes.

A particular place that is commonly selected by them to reside is areas with expanses of water, such as seas and oceans. Therefore it is significant that the Bermuda Triangle, which is infamous for mysterious occurrences that take place in the area, is actually the place with the largest inhabitation of Jinn because their government and administration is centered there. The residence of the king of the Jinn is also found in this place. It is from this center that the plans and decisions for any actions they carry out in the world are formulated.

With regard to reports of planes and ships mysteriously vanishing while crossing this supernatural place, the people aboard who disappear along with these vessels are still alive but living in another dimension, i.e., the world of Jinn. They are still human beings but with the difference that they possess the same characteristics and special abilities as the Jinn.

This raises the question as to how did they disappear in a split second without trace and without being discovered, despite years of investigation to search for them using the most up-to-date technology? There are two possible explanations. The first is that they do not know how to find a way out of the world of Jinn. The second is that they live a life of ease and comfort there, therefore it has not crossed their minds to leave that world.

Besides seas and oceans, cemeteries are another place where Jinn like to set up residence or even form a community. This is because among many beliefs that exist in the world, human beings always keep in mind a sense of respect and they are careful of their actions when they visit places of the dead.

When visiting cemeteries, certain etiquette should be observed. One should not remove plants or flowers that grow there, relieve oneself, nor harm or kill any animal that one comes across. These points should be kept in mind and not ignored because if one is in an unfavorable situation, the Jinn who inhabit these grounds will not allow the person who does not heed these points to simply depart.

Even among humankind, a person would surely take great exception if someone came to their house and deposited rubbish or relieved themselves in their compound, let alone if they entered their house and left it in a disorderly state. People who used to follow traditional cultural beliefs would be told to wash themselves and change their clothes after returning from a burial ground and, if possible, sprinkle salt over parts of their bodies in order to frighten the Jinn away.

There are many places where the Jinn have a particular preference to take up residence, many of which humankind would find abhorrent. Among such places, mortuaries are a favorite. The reasons they choose such places are difficult to understand.

Therefore it follows that persons who are employed in cemeteries or mortuaries are highly exposed to the possibility of interference or attack by Jinn. The emotional and psychological state of some individuals who have worked for long periods in these places can be quite puzzling. A faraway look in their eyes and their movements can be indicative of some mild form of emotional disturbance, although this does not apply to all of them.

Society in general tends to associate the strange illnesses that afflict individuals who are employed in cemeteries and mortuaries as stemming from their work, even if they have long since stopped working or retired from this form of employment. In the case of mortuaries, Jinn are not only found in the rooms where corpses are kept but they are also known to follow the mortuary vehicles.

Hearses or vehicles that transport the deceased to burial may also be the source that brings the risk of Jinn disturbance to their surroundings when they are parked in places inhabited by large populations, such as housing areas. It is also not impossible for someone who takes the chance of spending the night inside one of these vehicles to fall victim to a strange illness or mental problems, even resulting in death. Cars of ordinary individuals that have transported a corpse may also be at risk of misfortune at a time close after the incident.

Therefore, one should never show bravado by attempting to challenge the Jinn. Once they decide to do evil, they would not hesitate to kill a human being.

In addition to these places, mountains and highlands also constitute areas where Jinn commonly build their dwellings, not excluding forests and jungles as well. Therefore, it is not surprising that people of old who subscribed to traditional cultural beliefs would advise anyone who wished to go hunting not to enter the jungle alone in case they became lost due to trickery of the Jinn and subsequently could not find their way back, nor find anyone to guide them out of the jungle.

Moreover, the hustle and bustle of metropolitan cities crammed full of people and vehicles resulting in a clamor of deafening noise are also favored places of Jinn to inhabit, especially quiet, ill-kept alleys in between dark and empty buildings.

It follows that other favorite places of theirs to dwell are large houses or mansions, especially those that have had no inhabitants for long periods of time. This is why society in general— all over the world—assumes that places in which people have not lived for many years are haunted by ghosts of the dead. Places such as these that have been left empty for at least forty days may be visited by Jinn.

The author wishes to relate a true story regarding a house that was located near a city. The local people believed this particular house was haunted. It had previously been rented by a number of tenants who were taken by the house's attractive and luxurious look. Yet all of these tenants could not endure living in the house longer than five days. Eventually no one else desired to stay in the house, and it was left devoid of inhabitants.

Some time after, another family desired to rent the house as they liked its style and strategic location close to the city center. They had already been informed about the history of the house's previous inhabitants before they even knew about the frightening situations that had occurred inside its walls. Nevertheless, they just dismissed it as superstitious nonsense. The owner agreed to let them live there but he would not accept any payment, even though they insisted paying him rent.

The first night they spent in the house, something about its atmosphere made them feel uneasy. The following morning after they woke up, the husband and wife were horrified to find the two beds situated in their children's bedroom had somehow been thrown out of the window. Just as mystifying was the scene of their children still sound asleep on the bedroom floor.

Although the experience was a truly frightening one, they managed to put it out of their minds. Sadly, several days later tragedy struck. One morning, the couple woke to find the heart-wrenching scene of their beloved children lying dead outside the house as if they had been thrown out of the same window.

If anyone should be aware of any sign or indication of the presence of Jinn in their house or dwellings, they should move out as soon as possible. If these Jinn are trying to make their presence known, it means they are about to perpetrate some form of interference or disturbance. Alternatively, seek the assistance of someone who knows how to exorcise Jinn from houses or places.

Various mysterious stories

Cities and towns epitomize human life that never ceases activity with different people going hither and thither, busy and engrossed in their personal affairs and daily needs. Rarely are they ever aware that there is another form of life equally active, running here and there, attending to their own affairs that are not so unalike humankind's life in the real world.

These, of course, are the living beings of the unseen world.

Imagine an attractive-looking house located quite near to the center of one of these cities. In the compound are several stately-looking trees with a lush growth of leaves that almost covers the whole roof. This is a picturesque view of a beautiful house, pleasing to the eye. However, without people who live inside this house, the view suddenly becomes devoid of life and eerie.

A true story of a similar mysterious house happened whereby the new tenants were unaware of its previous history. One day, the mother was in the bedroom of her child of seven years old, who was always noticed laughing and playing with someone who could not be seen— a Jinn. The mother was startled by her child's continuous behavior of laughing and talking to something supposedly imaginary, so scolded the child. Suddenly a hand appeared from behind the bedroom door and scratched the woman's face until it bled. It was only then she became aware her child was playing with a Jinn. Not long after the family moved from the house.

After they vacated the house, it remained empty of tenants for several years. Following this, however, another family took up residence in the house.

The new tenants were a family of three; a couple with a young daughter. Approximately two weeks after they moved in, something began to disturb their daughter at night to the point where she would cry and could not sleep. She had previously told them about seeing a woman with long hair in the compound of their house. Following this incident, she would continuously fall sick off and on, as well as break into tears because she felt afraid.

The people were advised by a practitioner of spiritual power to move out, because their house had been taken over by a Jinn. If they continued to inhabit this place, great danger would come upon them. They were also told that their child would recover only after they left this house. When they moved to another residence, the child became well again within two months.

The house then remained empty for three months. When the new tenants wanted to take up residence, the owner informed them about the strange happenings there, but his advice fell on deaf ears.

The first time they stepped into the house and saw its condition, they assumed all the stories they had been told were fables and sheer nonsense. It was only after residing there for three weeks they began to noticed a change in the atmosphere of the house. The first sign was the sound of a piano in the middle of the night although nobody else was in the house besides them, but they did not give much thought to it. However, the same disturbance happened next night, and they started to become worried. On one particular night, the wife was out of the bedroom and the husband was sleeping alone. He clearly felt the sinking of the mattress on the other side of the bed as if someone were lying next to him.

After this occurrence the husband, wife, and child all slept in one room. They were clearly in a state of anxiety and began to make preparations to move.

Mysterious happenings at night

One night, a man was driving home when he suddenly noticed in the distance the outline of a woman trying to flag down his car for assistance. He stopped his car and obliged her with a lift, whereby she entered and sat in the back seat.

She then proceeded to tell him about the problems she was facing. She was clearly mixed-up, and her voice was hoarse and anxious as she explained her troubled, unhappy circumstances. The man then turned to look at her and was shocked to see the woman's face had changed into something macabre.

Suddenly, her head separated from her body and began to move disembodied towards the front passenger seat. Faced with this horrifying, abnormal situation, the man began to implore Allah with du'as and recite verses from the Qur'an, and forthwith the gruesome apparition vanished.

The man made his way home driving in a state of panic and terror. Not long after the incident, he was struck down with a mysterious illness that lasted several months and the cause of which was unknown. He did finally recover and according to the person who treated him, he had fallen victim to an attack by a Jinn on that fateful night.

In another story, a man was driving late during a very dark night, when suddenly before he could react he hit a motorcycle that seemed to come out of nowhere from the opposite direction. However, the truly puzzling aspect of the situation was that the moment after the crash, there were no signs to indicate that a collision had ever taken place. Cases such as these happen quite commonly, especially in quiet, isolated places in the middle of the night.

This is another form of Jinn disturbance carried out against human beings. These victims usually catch a glimpse of another person or vehicle, which causes them to stop or swerve suddenly. However, this results in some of them losing control, ending in an accident, such as their vehicle falling into a river or colliding with the road-divider. Nevertheless, at the time of the incident it is as if they see an object that is real but is in actual fact to the contrary.

In addition to accident cases such as those mentioned, there are also situations where someone is driving along a road that has only one lane in their direction, when suddenly they see the highway change into two or three lanes.

Moreover, the view in front of them suddenly becomes hazy and unclear, and they are unable to see the road. In that moment they panic and stop their car, and their vision returns to normal. There are also those who, while driving in the middle of the night, experience the sensation that their car is not moving or perhaps moving very slow as if it is has been loaded with something very heavy.

If we wished to investigate all forms of disturbance and despicable deeds carried out by Jinn against humankind, they would be far too many. In short, they use thousands of different ways and methods to spread their evil throughout the earth.

Mysterious places

It is common to hear of strange happenings at the scenes of fatal accidents whereby people claim to see the victims who died there suddenly appear or haunt the area. The same phenomena is also claimed to be witnessed at places where people had previously committed suicide or were victims of murder.

Cemeteries or burial grounds are places highly prone to settlement by Jinn. Therefore housing areas are not provided with the most favorable conditions when they are established near cemeteries. However, the situation becomes much more acutely dangerous when graves are transferred to different locations and a housing development takes place on cemetery land.

Any area located near or within burial land whereby the previous graves have been moved will not escape interference and attack by Jinn, and this will center on those inhabitants located in these areas.

In a situation such as this, interference and attack by Jinn present in these areas is very difficult to overcome. It will depend on the expertise of individuals experienced in exorcising Jinn from places where they cause trouble to the general public. Even if they manage to succeed, it will only occur after investing a great deal of time and effort to convince or drive the Jinn away from the affected place.

In fact, many eerie stories are heard pertaining to a small group of individuals who behave irresponsibly in these places. For example, what befell certain people who relieved themselves publicly in cemeteries. Some were struck down by mysterious illnesses that lingered for years and could not be treated by doctors.

Areas or places of residence where cases of mysterious deaths previously took place are highly susceptible to attract the unwanted attention of Jinn, such as where murders, suicides, and violent crimes resulting in the loss of life were involved. In short, any area where blood was spilt is at great risk of interference and attack by Jinn.

Normally, whenever Jinn show glimpses of their presence to humankind, it should be taken as a sign of danger and precautionary steps should be taken forthwith. The exception is where Jinn are being pursued or driven away by those skilled in the subtleties of the Jinn world.

This skill or experience depends on the religion of these individuals. In Islam, those who attempt to drive away Jinn normally use verses of the Qur'an and pray to Allah asking for help and strength. With His help, nothing is impossible because no matter how powerful the Jinn may be, they could never be able to stand up to Allah. Non-Muslims also have their own individual methods to remove supernatural beings.

It is quite startling that toilets are included among the favorite places of Jinn. There is a story of a man staying alone at a hotel who needed to use the toilet in his room. He was shocked to open his bathroom door and see someone else in there with a hideous face and long hair. The creature was a Jinn, and it bellowed at him to leave the bathroom immediately. The man was terrified and without hesitation he fled. As strange as the story sounds, it is not impossible.

Hospitals too have their own strange stories. In almost all hospitals, Jinn and devils will normally be found due to the many cases of death involving loss of blood, which is a favorite substance of the Jinn. If a place contains something that Jinn enjoy, they will not move from that location.

There are many unusual cases that have been related regarding happenings in hospitals, particularly those connected to deaths there.

In one particular incident, there was a patient who caught a glimpse of an indistinct, long-haired creature with hair all over its body that was licking blood that had spilt over the floor. Terrified, the patient called for the nurse, but she could not see anything unusual there.

In fact, not everyone will be able to see something that actually appears from the unseen world. This is because certain people reject and refuse to believe in supernatural happenings

MYSTERIOUS PHENOMENA OF THE UNSEEN WORLD

such as those mentioned. This becomes a barrier that prevents them from being able to witness these phenomena for themselves.

In addition, the maternity ward of a hospital is a place where a great deal of excess blood occurs in situations due to the process of childbirth. Therefore, it should come as no surprise that it is a place frequented by Jinn due to the blood that they seek as a source of food, although humankind cannot witness this for themselves.

Nurses on duty in maternity wards may find themselves smeared with blood when they are assisting mothers-to-be in giving birth. If they do not clean themselves after finishing their duties, it is not impossible that they could find themselves at risk from attack by Jinn. Usually, this type of disturbance can continue for a long time.

Generally, nurses are highly exposed to attack by Jinn. They may be struck down by forms of mysterious, unusual illnesses as a result of the negative effects of these attacks.

If employees of a mortuary were to be asked why they feel no fear while carrying out their duties, they would probably answer that these duties have become part of their normal working environment. However, they may be totally unaware that the risk of being subjected to attack by Jinn is very high.

It is imperative for such workers to be on their guard and take precautionary steps such as observing proper behavior and speech, so as not to invite anger and subsequent interference from the Jinn. It is estimated that twenty to thirty percent, or maybe more, of mortuary workers fall victim to Jinn disturbance, resulting in conditions such as mental problems and insanity.

This risk may also extend to workers such as grave-diggers. It is important for them to ensure they are in a clean and pure state before returning home after work, so as not to attract Jinn with them who may then select their family members as targets.

These workers are at equally high risk of interference as mortuary workers.

People should always be careful at places such as mortuaries that are holding the corpses of people yet to be claimed, as these buildings represent a familiar place for Jinn to set up home. Certain actions will attract the unfavorable attention of the Jinn and their anger, such as squeezing the juice out of lemons or the spraying of hot water. These two actions are hated by Jinn, and those doing them may risk being subjected to their interference.

Another location where people should be on their guard is prisons, especially the area that is reserved for executions. The atmosphere alone in such places is enough to cause fear and anxiety.

In addition slaughterhouses, where copious amounts of animal blood are continuously spilt, are places where the workers are at risk from interference.

Individuals personally involved with the execution of criminals represent one of those groups at the highest risk of disturbance and attack by Jinn. This is because the atmosphere surrounding incidents involving death or murder is one most liked by Jinn.

There is a heart-wrenching story concerning the effect of supernatural influence as a result of the process of execution of criminals. There was a man employed in carrying out the death penalty who suffered constant tragedy in his life when all six of his children were born handicapped.

The psychological effects from the burden of his work manifested themselves as extreme fear and anxiety. He constantly drank alcohol throughout the day due to the stress he felt as a result of his work in carrying out executions.

It would not be in the extreme to say that not less than thirty to forty percent of babies born handicapped are due to the interference of Jinn. Those who reflect deeply would not be bold enough to carry out duties such as those of the man previously mentioned due to the risk of the considerable burden that awaits them. No one could ever forget if they should witness the gruesome, terrified expression on the face of the deceased who has been executed.

There was a story of someone who played a joke by putting over his head a black hood that was previously used to cover the heads of people who were about to be put to death. He suddenly died soon after. Many believed it was on account of disturbance by an unseen being.

If this kind of hood was brought back to a person's home, it could bring a supernatural influence into the house causing the inhabitants to suffer from disturbance such as the hysteria and delirium in the middle of the night.

It would not be surprising if all places that have regularly witnessed death, murder, and the shedding of human blood should hold many mysteries connected to the unseen world.

The same applies to places that have witnessed the sacrifice of many human lives, such as the Twin Towers in the United States. The buildings constructed in their place are not safe and represent a great risk to local people because the location has probably become home to a community of Jinn.

It is certain that people who regularly go hunting in forests or jungles may have undergone some strange experiences there that rarely happen in other locations.

It may be supposed that the reason people become lost in forests or jungles is their lack of knowledge or unfamiliarity with the varying paths in and out of these areas.

Yet it cannot be denied that another reason they become lost may be solely due to the Jinn selecting them as a target for their amusement and interference, in such a way that their vision becomes indistinct even through they are totally familiar with the paths that lead in and out of a particular forest or jungle.

It is not impossible for people who become an object of the Jinn's entertainment and disturbance—let alone in the forest or jungle—to become lost even when making their way back home via familiar routes. There are others who become lost to the point they enter the Jinn's world. When they are eventually found, they may display symptoms of an unstable mental state or fall sick to mysterious conditions that could be fatal.

People who are fond of furnishing their houses with earthenware or statues made out of iron or wood—particularly those of the color black—should also beware that these objects are common hiding places for Jinn and devils.

They have a greater preference for statues that have been formed with complete features and true representation. The same applies to portraits and large pictures of people hung on the walls of houses.

Even supposing one is not impressed or does not approve of the form or look of a statue, it should not be disposed of by burning. This is a precaution in case there may be a Jinn residing inside it, who may then react by attacking and causing disturbance in one's daily life.

The risks arising from attack by Jinn are extremely perilous because they normally cause the individual concerned to fall seriously ill. It is not impossible that the pain and suffering resulting from this could cause the individual to pass away suddenly.

If we reflect on the issues discussed so far, we may wonder just how many people have fallen victim or even been sacrificed due to the evil of interference and attack by Jinn and devils. Indeed, in the outside world, there are still many human beings at constant risk due to carelessness and ignorance in facing these supernatural creatures. Only Allah truly knows.

Conclusion

Let us conclude with a summary of everything we have learned up to this point. The existence of Jinn is a true reality that cannot be denied, despite the inability of humankind to perceive their presence by the normal human senses because they belong to the unseen world.

Almost all aspects of human existence in this realm are inextricably intertwined with them. If humankind should experience unusual moments in their lives, it is not improbable that Jinn may be the root cause.

Everywhere in our world today, we can see with our own eyes the ruination wreaked by them. If it were not for the protection of Allah, it would have been totally impossible for humankind to live this far and avoid extinction. Their existence is acknowledged by almost every religion and belief throughout the whole world, although they are designated by various different names.

The world, however, is continually in a state of confusion regarding the true reality of Jinn and considers them creatures such as aliens from outer space in UFOs. Yet the Jinn are no more than a species of being created by Allah who live alongside human beings sharing the same time and space. They possess a *ruh* (spirit), rational mind, feelings, and emotions in the same way as humankind, and moreover have their own individual system of society. They possess many more abilities and advantages than humankind.

It we look at it from the perspective of children, their powers are far stronger than all the superheroes in the world combined such as *Superman, the Incredible Hulk, Spiderman, the X-Men, Batman* and others. It is imperative to remember that they should never be challenged. If success is not on the human's side, the price to pay from such a conflagration would be insurmountably high, involving a matter of life and death for them and possibly even their family.

In fact, it is intended that much more be presented on the subject for the reader's interest, and this effort will be continued in a subsequent book. The author hopes that this story will not be considered just as mere entertainment, but a significant effort in attempting to illustrate some of the true circumstances of what is meant by the unseen world as well as beneficial learning for each and every one.